From The Inside Looking Out

Glen R. Reed Jr.

Fulton Books, Inc.
Meadville, PA

Published by Fulton Books 2020

ISBN 978-1-64654-518-6 (paperback)
ISBN 978-1-64654-886-6 (hardcover)
ISBN 978-1-64654-798-2 (digital)

Printed in the United States of America

CONTENTS

PREFACE

One could ask what goes on between the thick walls and the razor concertina wire fences of the penitentiary. What actually goes on is not what you have been told, heard, or have observed on most movies or television programs. What goes on inside the penitentiary will stay within the penitentiary. I personally believe the most accurate portrayal of the penitentiary life is the classic movie *The Shawshank Redemption* in 1994 with actors Morgan Freeman and Tim Robbins. But remember, this classic screenshot is only a movie.

Your imagination compiled with outside influence can give you a general perspective of what goes on the inside walls of the penitentiary. However, nothing on television or anything that has been told is further from the truth concerning the life in the penitentiary.

It is evident that to fully comprehend the entire picture of the inside of the penitentiary, an individual would have had been incarcerated at some point in their life and had been employed by the system to fully understand. In the following pages of this book, I will spell out what I have observed with my own eyes over the many years I was employed as a correctional officer on what takes place on the inside of the penitentiary. Sit back, take a deep breath, and let's take a journey down this dark and dreary road of "looking from the inside out."

ACKNOWLEDGMENTS

I thank my Christian wife for her vast amount of godly wisdom, counsel, and extreme dedication in raising our two boys. Without her amazing advice and her God-fearing criticism, the ability to write this book would have been impossible. Thank you, my wonderful wife. You are the apple of *my* eye.

I thank both of my sons, Steven and David, for giving me the opportunity to be your dad, although I feel I let you down several times over the years for not being there when I should have been. I want you to know that I did my best. I love both of you very much.

I thank David May, my brother in Christ, for sharing the gospel of Jesus Christ with me. Due to his love of Jesus, I accepted Christ into my life, and until this day, the Word of God has allowed me to fully understand what is important in this short span of life on earth.

I thank Don Francisco (Flute4Jesus), who spent thirty years of his life in the military serving God and country. His steadfast belief in Jesus Christ is the strongest of any individual I have ever had the opportunity to know.

I thank Art Garrett, my friend who is also retired from the United States Marine Corps and who understands the reason I am writing this book due to his career within the Department of Corrections.

I thank Officer Steven Cobb, Officer Danielle Wrencher, and Officer Alina McCray, three of the finest correctional officers I had the opportunity to work with on a daily basis. Without their everyday support and protection of one another's back, it would have been impossible to handle the unexpected on a daily basis and have the assurance we went home safe to our families.

I thank Officer Richard Wilkie, who walked more miles on M-N-O yards during the past twelve years than I have on my Toyota pickup truck—tremendous endurance for an individual who made the safety of all staff his main priority

I thank my wonderful parents, Thad and Barbara Baker, for raising me right and always being there when I needed them. I surely miss them both every day.

I thank the Department of Correction and the Department of Public Safety for their support. I was associated with some of the finest correctional personnel, I believe, in the prison system.

And finally, I must ultimately thank this great country of ours for allowing me the privilege and honor to serve and protect it for over twenty years as a member of the armed forces of the greatest nation in the world, the United States of America.

INTRODUCTION

It was a beautiful day in May 1991. The sun was bright, and I was on my way to obtain my final discharge out of the US Army. I walked into Building T-61 on Fort McClellan, Alabama. I was on my way to the military retirement section to officially end a wonderful twenty-year military career. My only thoughts at that particular time were completing my out-processing paperwork, clearing my government quarters inspection, signing off post, and driving back home to the beautiful state of North Carolina.

After officially completing all the final requirements, I immediately loaded my family in the car and began the drive home when, suddenly, my mind began to wander all over the place. It dawned on me that I had been secure the past twenty years in the military with a steady income and permanent job. That was rewarding and satisfying and, most of all, guaranteed me a monthly check for my wife and for our two sons.

Wow, it hit me like a ton of bricks. Guess what, dummy! You are unemployed. What are you going to do now? How are you going to support your family on such a small, insufficient retirement check?

As the days went by, I found a small part-time job and applied for schooling at the local community college in

Fayetteville, North Carolina, under the GI Bill. This helped support my family, and we were able to survive on more of a fixed income. But I prayed, and continued to pray, that something would come along that was more financially stable for us and, at the same time, what I would enjoy doing. I immediately applied for civil service at Fort Bragg, North Carolina; however, they were not hiring at the time. Then the light bulb came on. I told myself, "You spent all those years in the military. Why not use this experience and knowledge in your search for better employment?"

I had a military police background as a military police-man in the service as my secondary military occupation, so I applied for several law enforcement positions in all the sur-rounding communities and counties. I eventually received a response later that the North Carolina Department of Correction (DOC) was hiring and that if you have had any background, you should apply. I filled out an application, and within a few months, I was called in for an interview with the local prison in our area.

Approximately two months later, I received a certi-fied letter from the Department of Correction for a second interview at the same location. Within a month, I inter-viewed again for the position of a correctional officer. I was accepted by the prison.

They made me an appointment for a medical, physical, and mental evaluation and a criminal background check.

When these requirements came back in good stand-ing, I was informed to report for my first day of work on a Monday morning at 8:00 a.m. This day I will never forget; it was the seventh day of June 1992.

I began to work and, within a few months, was sent to the correction officers basic course in Wilmington, North Carolina, located on Kure Beach (Fort Fisher) next to the Atlantic Ocean. The total course was six weeks in length. Upon graduating from school, I began working in the prison, no longer requiring another officer as an escort because I was certified by the State of North Carolina. I was on my own and totally responsible for my own actions as an officer. The next day, as I entered the main prison gate, I heard the electric gate slam shut, and then and only then did I realize I was locked up on the inside. Little did I know what I was stepping into.

After looking back twenty-two years and trying to figure out why things in the prison are the way they are, I have come to this conclusion. This is why I am sharing my personal experiences and explaining to everyone what really goes on behind the fences and the razor wire of the prison.

First of all, prison is a very diverse and unique community of its own. It is a community setting that has its own set of rules guided by an approved set of policies and procedures, an area that is mostly secluded from main society and is in most instances out of sight of normal everyday public activities.

However, this small diverse community houses some of the most dangerous, evil, ruthless, and heinous individuals known to our society. These individuals referred to as convicts and inmates are placed here by the court systems for crimes they have been found guilty of, some for the rest of their natural life. This entire area is surrounded by miles of long double fences with razor wire rolled on the ground and on the top of every inch of fence. The entire area has several gun towers on all the corners and on the sides with each tower having a correctional officer assigned with ammunition and weapons in their possession.

These weapons on these towers were a single-barrel pump shotgun, Smith & Wesson .357 Magnum pistol, M&P .40-caliber pistol, and a Ruger Mini-14 rifle. Seem a little much but are effective in keeping the inmate or convict inside and not allowing them to escape in order to protect the safety of the general public. Since my leaving the prison, the towers have been removed, and an electronic fence has replaced the towers with roving patrols around the parameter of the prison.

This is effective but not as effective as eyes on all areas of the fence line at all times.

The number of inmates and convicts housed on the inside of these prisons differ due to the size and location of the prison.

The entire prison is manned 24 hours a day, 7 days a week, and 365 days per year, referred to as 24/7. And what goes on behind these fences and the razor wire normally stays there. However, I want everyone to know and understand what it is like "looking from the inside out."

CHAPTER 1

Neither Judge nor Jury
Be Fair but Firm

It was 3:15 a.m., and my alarm clock was sounding reveille, letting me know it was time to jump up and prepare for another day at work. Being extremely tired, I forced myself out of bed and wandered straight to the bathroom for my morning shower. I put on my uniform, packed lunch, and poured myself a large cup of black coffee. With my coffee cup in hand, I started on the twenty-two-mile commute to my destination.

The drive seemed longer than normal that morning, for I was daydreaming of what the day might be like when I arrive. The fog that morning was extra heavy, so I drove extremely slow on the dark backcountry roads. I honestly believe all deer and all of God's creatures loved to stare into the headlights of my vehicle every morning. One would believe they were waiting to personally greet me each and every morning. Upon arriving in the prison parking lot, I would begin my day by physically checking my pockets and personal belongings to ensure I did not possess any items as my cell phone, pocket knife, or tobacco, which were not authorized inside the prison.

When I arrived at the main gate entrance, the shift officer on the gate would ask to see my identification card and credentials and complete an electronic paddle-search of my body and inspect my personal items prior to authorizing my entrance. This procedure was frustrating but was necessary to ensure that no unauthorized contraband was being allowed inside the prison. A more simplified and effective system could have been implemented. The procedure was discomforting because we were required to remove our coats, belt, and boots; empty our pockets; and turn them all inside out. The problem officers and staff had with this procedure was due to the adverse weather conditions outside. If the temperature happened to be freezing—ice or snow—you were still required to remove your coats, gloves, belt, and boots and empty your pockets.

This requirement was always conducted outside of the building in a small sally port with little to no protection from the wind or the outside elements of the weather. Most staff complained and submitted many suggestions to the superintendent, captains, and the lieutenants; however, it was like talking to a brick wall. This seemed unjustified and unfair to the officers and staff because the inmates were always allowed to be inside where they were never subjected to the outside elements for searches. It was pretty obvious their safety and welfare were placed above ours.

Upon finishing the entry procedure to the facility, we all assembled in a small room adjacent to the lieutenant's office referred to as the lineup room. This was where the oncoming shift lieutenant would discuss all possible problems or pertinent information to all the staff prior to going on shift. The room was not very large with several chairs lined up around the walls. We were required to stand during this time with our hats on our heads. The lineup normally took fifteen minutes in order for us to relieve the outgoing shift on time. It amazed me and the staff that the unit would use some of this important time to bring in vendors from the community, such as insurance agents from outside to offer us more insurance.

This delay would take longer than normal and sometimes caused us to be late relieving the outgoing shift. During lineup and other activities, the captain, lieutenant, or the sergeant would announce all work assignments for each officer in the lineup. We normally had less than forty officers per shift to control and provide security to an inmate population near one thousand. This was a poor *officer to inmate ratio* considering how extremely dangerous this job could become in the blink of an eye.

If a fight, disturbance, or assault erupted in an area with only a few officers present, this situation could become out of control before other officers came running to the scene for assistance.

If more officers were assigned to each work position, the situation could quickly be controlled and possibly without injury.

Early one morning, I was assigned to the ABCD dormitories. I just completed the morning count of all inmates in the dorms and relayed the inmate count to master control. While in the process of inventorying all security equipment for shift change—handcuffs, leg cuffs, black security boxes, flashlights, water shutoff keys, batons, and radios—it was announced over the unit PA system that all areas needed to conduct an immediate recount of all inmates in the prison. This, by far, was the one most important aspect of our job—to ensure that there is an accurate count of all inmates assigned in our area. If the count does not clear *over the entire prison*, all things are placed on immediate shutdown, and neither shift coming on duty or leaving was allowed to exit the prison until the unit count was corrected and cleared. This was not an unusual occurrence, for recounts happen in the prison environment quite frequently. Recounts are necessary due to security reasons. This procedure required by policy was necessary to ensure that at no given time were any inmate(s) unaccounted for due to possible escapes, transfers, hospital visits, work assignments (such as in the kitchen), or for any other reason. Recounts were often performed because inmates love to play cat-and-mouse games with the staff. Inmates would often hide during these counts just for the fun of it, knowing it caused staff problems. They would be given a write-up if it was proven they did it on purpose. This was quite difficult to prove most of the time. Official counts were completed at least three times per day and more if the need arose.

The count finally did clear. All security equipment was accounted for, and the normal operations of the day began. In the next few minutes, the officer assigned to feed would start to call inmates to the dining facility for the breakfast meal. Each dorm was called to the dining facility until the entire inmate population had been fed. This also included all special-diet inmates who normally ate first or last.

The entire feeding process normally took a little over one hour if the dining facility did not run out of the proper amount of prepared food. This happened on a regular basis. Inmate cooks prepared and cooked all the food for every meal served. To the inmate, it was no problem to be slow or to prepare food for inadequate or improper preparation because they felt they had all the time in the world, and we the staff were on their time schedule. The main cooks usually had pride in their work; however, the average cook and dining facility worker did not want to be in the kitchen, and this was evident in their behavior and attitude every day. The dining facility manager had a difficult time trying to keep good cooks and kitchen workers at all times. He spent more of his time hiring and firing inmates in the kitchen on a daily basis. Inmates were master thieves and notorious for stealing anything that was not tied down. The dining facility manager was always writing reports on inmates and placing them in segregation for stealing food and other items from the dining facility. The dining facility was often referred to as the house of thieves.

Upon the completion of feeding breakfast and if the weather was normal and visibility was given a green light by the officers on all manned gun towers, the yards were opened for the inmates to go outside on the yards to purchase items from the canteens and for recreational purposes.

When inmates had completely exited the dorms to the yards for recreation, schools, and jobs, the assigned dorm janitors for each dorm would begin to clean the showers, bathrooms, sleeping areas, and hallways and empty the trash. That particular morning, I noticed a dorm janitor lying on his bed and not cleaning his assigned dorm area as he was required. I approached him and asked him why he was lying down and not cleaning on his assigned job.

His response to me was he did not feel like it and that he was not going to clean or do anything today. I again explained to him in a fair but firm manner that he needed to start cleaning. He became agitated and started using vulgar profanity, shouting out loudly. He then made the mistake of telling me he was not working for the second time. He then explained to me that he was in prison for a life sentence without the possibility of parole, and nothing, including me, was going to make him do anything. I again explained to him in a normal tone of voice that disobeying an order would only make his time harder and that he should think before he makes bad decisions.

He then stated, "Let me tell you something. You all locked me up for life without parole and put me here." I had heard enough! I quickly warmed to the subject at hand. I immediately placed the inmate in restraints (handcuffs) and explained the facts of life to him like a father would to his child. I wanted him to fully understand where I was coming from, so I had him sit in a chair, and I started to explain to him where I was coming from. I told him, "It was your decision to carry out the crime you committed. I was not present. The family members of your victim[s] who you mentally hurt were not there. Your life sentence belongs to you and you only. No one else. You must learn to accept and do your time. No one can or will do it for you. The sooner you realize your life sentence belongs to you and no one else, the sooner you will be able to adjust and deal with it.

"As far as your life sentence without parole is concerned, I want you to understand that I had nothing to do with it. You can only blame yourself. Your amount of time is your time. I did not give it to you. I was not on your jury, and I certainly was not your judge. However, in the position as a correctional officer, I am not here to punish you for your crime. The courts have already done that, but I am here to ensure you abide by the policy and procedures of this prison, abide by the rules and regulations, and extend protection and safety for you at all times."

In a few minutes, as he sat and stared at the wall, he started to de-escalate and, in a normal tone of voice, asked me if I was going to write him up on a report and place him in segregation for disobeying an order. I could have locked him up for violations of disobeying an order, stopping work, and using profanity towards a correctional officer. As a correctional officer, you must learn to be "firm but fair." I informed him that I was going to give him a warning at this time on the condition that he not cause any more issues and he complete his assigned duties, but I also at the same time was very determined to drive my point home. I informed him that I needed him to think hard concerning our conversation today and the consequences that he could face for that type of unacceptable behavior. I explained to him that respect is not given; it is earned. He nodded his head and, without hesitation, stood up. I removed his restraints, and he went straight back to his dorm and cleaned up as required. I never had an issue with this particular inmate again; however, there were many more like him in prison who needed to understand that the officers and the correctional staff were not there to punish them. They had been punished already. Their time in prison belonged to them and them only, and it was up to each of them to deal with it, for we, as the correctional officers, were not the 'judge nor jury.'

CHAPTER 2

Snitches, Bitches, and Stiches

No one in their wildest imagination can fully understand what disgusting and unbelievable events take place on a day-to-day basis within the razor wire fences of a prison. You would have had to work in this environment to fully comprehend what I am going to discuss in this chapter. Although these are, for the most part, gross, nasty, and disgusting, please do not take offense, for it is the way of life in the penitentiary.

It has been often said, "What goes on inside the prison stays in the prison." This needs some discussion because it's your hard-earned tax dollars that are paying for the housing, food, clothing, education, fuel for transportation, and the enormous cost of medical services for the incarcerated individual. When you combine the total payroll for correctional officers and all correctional staff to include unnecessary expenditures, the amount is astronomical. The cost is being squeezed out of your—the citizens'—pockets. The prison is considered one of the most dangerous environments to work or live in because you are subjected to dangerous individuals who possess a variety of mental health issues and medical diagnosis, such as tuberculosis, HIV, AIDS, hepatitis, and other diseases transmitted by sexual activity and drugs.

It was bright outside and extremely hot that day. I was assigned as the yard officer for K and L dorms.

After completing my security check, the yards were opened for use by the inmates. Upon entering the front of K building, I observed an extremely large line of inmates standing and sitting around the picnic table. Some were rapping lyrics of songs, laughing, and what appeared to be having normal conversations among themselves. The canteen (commissary) in front of L dorm was lined up with inmates waiting to purchase their personal and food items, such as sodas, candies, chips, sandwiches, radios, batteries, and hygiene products.

I would like to put this in perspective before I go any further. I was the only correctional officer assigned to these two yards at this time. There were approximately 150 inmates on the yard. It was my sole responsibility to watch for possible signs that would be of concern, such as unauthorized gambling, disturbances, or a fight about to break out. I had established communication over the radio with the gun tower on the back of K yard.

Everything was calm and seemed very normal. Most disturbances, fights, and gang-related issues were active volcanoes just waiting to erupt and explode at any time.

As I turned to look toward the inmates around the picnic table, a fight broke out in the canteen (commissary line). I immediately called a code over the radio per policy and procedures for a disturbance or fight. I then observed an inmate in front of the line turn around and hit another inmate in the mouth. At this time, officers arrived from other locations to assist me, and the situation was controlled before it got further out of hand. The yards were immediately closed, and all inmates were directed back to their perspective dorms. With the assistance from another officer, we attempted to help the inmate on the ground on his feet. He was bleeding from his mouth and crawling around in the dirt. Both of his front teeth were knocked out by the other inmate, and his radio broke into pieces on the ground in front of the canteen. Medical was immediately called, and the nurse on duty responded to the scene. Both inmates involved were placed in restraints (handcuffs) and escorted to medical for further evaluation. The inmate who hit the other inmate in the mouth had no visible cuts, bruises, scratches, or redness on neither his hands nor his arms. This led us to believe that he possibly hit the other inmate with something other than his fist or hands. This was usual practice in prison setting. The use of an item or homemade weapon is a concern for staff and the administration. You could conduct a complete search of the inmates to include all prison areas and never find all these weapons. No weapon or hard object was found or confiscated in the area where the fight erupted. The item possibly used was obviously passed off to another inmate who hid or got rid of it. Inmate deception is remarkable. Inmates usually use another inmate as a spy to watch for staff in order to carry out their deceptive acts of assaults, stealing, tattooing, and passing of contraband at the right time or moment to ensure there is no trail of evidence to be found.

This inmate is referred to as the *hawk*. The internal investigation conducted did not prove that an object was used in this particular fight. The reason he was found guilty of this assault and placed in segregation was I was fortunate enough to have witnessed the entire incident. Both inmates were placed in segregation after their medical screening, pending outcome of the investigation. The inmate who was assaulted was transported outside the prison on a medical trip to a dentist for further necessary treatment on his mouth and teeth.

Again, additional medical bills at the cost of the taxpayer! Could this assault have been prevented if the proper staffing had been on the yard? Probably not. However with proper staffing, the odds would have been better. Within a short period of time, the lieutenant confirmed the reason the inmate was assaulted. It was due to the inmate being a known *snitch* who was known for talking to staff and feeding sensitive information concerning the movement of drugs and other contraband within the prison. This was a sure indicator that this inmate was an absolute snitch. If you were a snitch or had been labeled as a snitch, there was no distinction between the two as far as the other inmates were concerned. Just the smallest rumor that an inmate could be a snitch carried the same weight and consequences as if you were known for snitching.

Both were detrimental to one's well-being.

Why then snitch? This is a fact of life in prison, and there are several reasons for this particular type of self-destructive behavior.

A snitch and/or a sex offender are spineless cowards not worthy and definitely not assets to the inmate population.

The snitch is on a self-destructive mission to attempt to make things easier on themselves.

A large percentage of snitches fall into the lifestyle of homosexuality. I cannot overemphasize the potential problems that can be detrimental to a snitch. They usually end up being assaulted, being hurt, and even possibly being killed. "If you snitch, you will end up with a stich." Snitches engage in this unpredictable behavior for the craziest reasons. They will snitch in order to obtain special favors from other inmates, extra food from staff, extra canteen, shorter time in segregation, and being assigned to the bed and dormitory of their choice. These are extremely popular payoffs for snitching if you live the life of a homosexual because a homosexual desires to be taken care of and being protected by their *sugar daddy*, who usually refers to the homosexual as their *state girl* or their *bitch*.

I was preparing to have all the inmates sent outside for recreation when a young inmate approached me and asked if he could speak to me in a private setting. I had him go to the sergeant's office at the back of the dormitory. We went in the office where he sat down and asked me for my assistance. His request was he wanted me to provide him a dorm janitor or yard janitor job. Jobs were not always available and normally paid only forty cents per day but were difficult to obtain.

I informed him I understood, and I would place his name on a waiting list along with all the other names on the list. I told to him that when the next opening came up, he would be considered along with the others on the list who have also requested this job. He then went there—snitch mode 101. He asked me if I was aware of the amount of contraband, such as marijuana, postal stamps, tattooing, gambling, and other items, being moved around in the prison. He wanted this job to the extent that he was willing to snitch out others even with the possibility of getting hurt. I knew this was an issue for his safety, so I had to be extremely careful in my handling of this sensitive matter. However, at the same time, I wanted to know where the contraband was coming from. I listened completely to what he was trying to offer me. He told me, giving me the information that was worth the job.

Before he left the office, I informed him that I could not promise him anything because I was not authorized to do so. I did, however, let him know that he was playing a very dangerous game that does have severe consequences and that he should refrain from such practices in the future. The information he provided me was as smoke in the wind and nothing else. The sad question about this type of situation and many others was, How long could he snitch before he got a stich? It did not take long.

Within a few months, this same inmate was assaulted and had to be transferred to another location for his own protection. To see a young man who had been assaulted was not a pretty sight. However, the snitch could only blame himself. He knew better but would always take the chance.

Inmates lived by a set of rules: "the inmate code of ethics."

These standards or rules were set deep in stone and were not meant to be broken. If they were broken by an inmate, they normally found themselves broken.

There were several indicators that inmates use in order to determine or verify if one was a snitch, a narc, or a pigeon. A few indicators are as follows:

1. You were considered a loner and a pushover and did not fit into the established system by all other inmates. This includes conversing with staff too much on a daily basis.
2. You had your time cut short in segregation and did not have to complete the entire punishment you received for your prison violation, such as extra duty.
3. You heard an inmate's name being announced over the PA system in excess.
4. You received special favors from any staff member.
5. You received extra items, such as canteen, radio, and hygiene products, when they knew you were an indigent.
6. You were labeled as a homosexual.

Many believe that being a snitch, narc, or pigeon was a lucrative business in prison. I had never, in over twenty-two years as a correctional officer, ever seen a "rich snitch," only a "foolish" one.

CHAPTER 3

Danger Ahead!
The Dining Facility

By far without question, the prison dining facility is the most dangerous place in the entire prison setting. This is the last place you want fights, disturbances, or major uprisings to occur. The dining facility maintains one the largest numbers of inmates at any one time in a controlled area. This setting takes place three times every day. Breakfast is normally served at 6:00 a.m., lunch at 11:00 a.m., and dinner at 4:00 p.m. Extreme caution is at the highest-level during meal-feeding times because of the type of environment. The inmates use this time to obtain extra food, steal food and condiments, barter, and trade for their profit. Inmates always gripe and complain on a continuous basis, especially concerning the type, taste, and quality of food they were being served. It is an impossible task to satisfy one inmate, let alone nearly one thousand, in a short one-hour time frame. For reasons unknown, the food does not agree to their taste buds, the food seems cold, their desired portion is too small, and they do not approve of the meal selection set forth by the prison master menu.

The dining facility is centrally located in the middle of the prison, set apart and fenced in separately from all other areas for the sole purposes of receiving food supplies and extra security.

The dining facility on the inside is split down the middle with a large four-foot concrete barrier wall between the east and west sides. The serving lines on both sides of the barrier serve the same type of food, with the only exception of medically controlled special diets. The dining area is furnished with stainless steel tables with the capacity to sit four inmates at one time. The table and chairs are mounted and secured to the floor. Inmates entering the dining facility for chow have their prison ID card swiped in the dining facility computer system by officers working on both sides. This is required for two reasons. The first is to ensure that proper head count is completed to record the exact number of meals being served, and the second reason is to ensure inmates do not switch sides of the dining facility in an attempt to consume an additional meal. Inmates are habitual complainers; they complain about the food but will steal or fight to obtain a double portion.

It's an unexplainable game they play, and it makes no sense. However, this is the prison environment, and there are no logical explanations why they think or act in this manner. After having their card swiped into the computer, they move up one at a time to the serving line. The serving line is where they receive their individual food tray. Upon my arrival in the prison, the trays were made of metal, but for good reasons, they were changed to plastic trays. The serving line is uniquely designed with an opening at the bottom of the long stainless steel serving counter approximately ten to twelve inches where their tray is passed through to them. They have no physical contact with the cooks or access to the food being served.

They are able to see the inmate cook on the other side, serving their food, but cannot physically control the amount being placed on their tray. The amount of food placed on an inmate's tray is required to be equally the same. For example, an inmate has one hamburger with bun, one desert, one vegetable, and one serving of french fries. Several times during feeding, a tray will purposely be passed out with two or more hamburgers with an extra serving of french fries. The officer assigned to observe the serving line will have the tray with extra food returned to the dining facility manager, and the inmate will be given a new tray with the proper amount of food. All inmates involved in this incident risk have the possibility of being written up for a violation and possibly being placed in segregation, pending on the outcome of an investigation.

The inmate cooks on the serving line will give out extra food for several reasons, usually because he owes a favor for his own selfish or financial gain, has a gambling debt, or has been threatened, and even for disgusting sexual favors.

There are normally four officers or less working the dining hall for all three meals. I have personally worked the dining hall when only three officers were present. This was the administration's normal practice. This again goes back to the problem of manpower shortage of correctional staff.

This makes your job more intense and frustrating as you are always waiting for the worst situation to happen.

Somewhere within the prison administration, it is conceived that taking the risk of someone getting hurt or possibly killed rather than properly staffing the prison is a chance they were willing to take. The same excuse was always about not enough money.

Several times, when an officer was hurt, it ended of up in the local court system and the administration being sued for inadequate staffing and protection for the officer who got hurt. One would have to ask, What is the value of protection, safety, and life of the correctional staff and the safety of the public? I personally believe they could care less as long as things ran smoothly in the prison. Many incidents in this setting could have been stopped before they started if proper staffing was assigned to the prison, especially in the dining facility during meals.

A larger portion of food being given to an inmate was usually stopped but not enough to brag about. The amount of food being taken from the dining facility to the yards or to the dorms was a constant issue seven days a week. It was never unusual to find food, coffee, apples, and oranges hidden in their wall lockers, pillowcases, boots, on their bodies, trash cans, under their clothing, or even inside their bodies. I had even found drinks and food inside the toilets. I will discuss this in a later chapter.

The worst scenario for a disturbance or a fight to break out would be in the main cooking area of the dining facility, especially during feeding of the meal. Inmates had access to all types of cooking utensils, such as knives, large spatulas, large metal spoons, large aluminum paddles, and many heavy aluminum and stainless steel pots in their work area. These tools were kept secured in a locked container and placed on a shadow board for visibility at all times.

One particular day, a metal spatula came up missing in the kitchen. The whole prison was placed on lockdown, and an immediate facility search was implemented. The spatula was never found. This could be a devastating situation resulting in a lot of injuries to the inmates and staff if not handled quickly and properly. For example, a large pot of hot boiling water or another type of liquid thrown on someone would be serious enough to cause major burns and injuries, not to mention the possibility of scaring for the rest of the individual's life if they survived this assault. However, most fights in the dining area were between the inmates. Fights would start due to an inmate taking food from a weaker inmate's tray or the tremendous heat in the kitchen. It involved certain gang-related (STG, special threat groups) groups sitting together and taking food from others' trays. Inmates were prohibited from passing food from tray to tray or give their food to another inmate, but this occurred constantly even with cameras monitoring the feeding. With only a few officers in the dining hall, it was difficult, but that was due to not having enough eyes looking to stop their manipulating tactics before they got started.

It always amazed me that they complained about the food and the amount they received. If you were to go and visit your children or grandchildren at their local schools and see what type of meals they received, you would be devastated and shocked.

The meals inmates receive in the prison environment are far better than what is provided for you children in the local public schools. It is a crying shame. It's unthinkable but a fact that convicted felons are eating better and healthier than your children at school.

What is chicken day? When the prison served chicken, they never had enough chicken to feed the entire population. They would always run out of chicken. Not enough chickens in the barn. The last dorm to eat would usually end up eating a substitute meal of beef patties or something that could be prepared quickly. The chicken thieves were out and were scouring up on every opportunity to steal the feathers right off the chicken before it was even cooked. It did not matter if you placed more staff on the yards, did more pat-down searches, or only fed a few at a time; chicken managed to get stolen all the time. I had personally found large bags of hot cooked chicken wrapped in plastic wrap inside a large garbage can. This would to be picked up later by another inmate. Chicken was a high commodity. It is an inmate treat to barter with, trade for other items, mix with ramen noodles, pay off, or used for all types of special favors.

Chicken to an inmate is one of his greatest assets even if it cost him several days in segregation or a bloody nose. All this for a piece of yard bird! Chicken cooked or not cooked had been found wrapped up in clear plastic and hid in the ceilings of the dining facility and, yes, even in the bathroom stalls and toilets of the dorms.

This may seem gross and sickening, but to an inmate, it was an acceptable practice and a justifiable trade-off for their own selfish reasons.

At the back of the kitchen on the loading dock, excess food scraps were placed into large galvanized trash cans. After each meal, at least two inmates were allowed outside on the back-loading dock to place all the food scraps into these cans. These scraps on a weekly basis would be picked up by a local hog farmer, who loaded them into a large container on his truck and trailer. One day, I asked the gentleman what he did with these scraps. He told me that he recooked the scraps, added some supplements, and then fed them to his hogs. When the hogs got to their proper weight, he then would sell them to the local meat slaughterhouses. These trash containers contained such a large amount of food.

What a waste. As an example, I observed this occurrence in the dining facility with my own eyes.

An inmate is required by policy and his right to be given three meals a day. It was not unusual to see inmates get their food trays and then immediately turn around and dump the whole thing into the trash. If they did not approve of the food being served, it was their right to throw it away because they had to be served a meal by law. This was their way of demonstrating their dislike for the food. If one hundred inmates discarded their tray three times per day, you could imagine what was thrown out for the hogs. It was a total waste of edible food and was unfortunate for all those paying taxes—a total system of waste and abuse that should be fixed.

At the back of the kitchen, the cooks prepared special dishes for themselves. For example, they have fried eggs, omelets, and French toast, and the general population got scrambled eggs. This was allowable. It may be a fringe benefit, but it kept them working and created a workable atmosphere. Being a cook had its advantages. It was always in the best interest for everyone that there was peace in the dining facility and not become a potential battlefield.

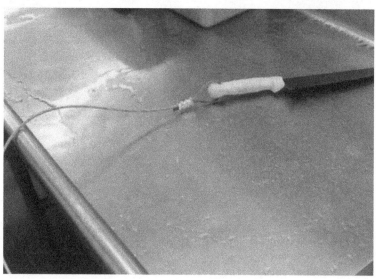

CHAPTER 4

When to Hold Them and When to Fold Them

Inmates are opportunists and will take the chance to end up on top of anything they put their deviant minds and greedy hands on. It is without question that an inmate will take any risk to gain substantial profit through others even though the risk could be detrimental to themselves or others. This self-imposed drive of uncontrollable greed and relentless thrill pushes them to the end of no limit. This is why *gambling* will always be a way of life for those incarcerated. Gambling can be defined as a conscious and deliberate effort to place valuables, usually but not always money, on how some event happens to turn out. For many years, gambling in prison has multiplied and evolved into a bloodthirsty ritual coveted by each and every inmate. Inmates will continue this pattern of greed and corruption in the penitentiaries, for they have found something they all thrive for.

The number of dorms in the prison I worked was twenty-eight, and each housed thirty-four to forty-two inmates per dorm. The prison had two segregation units capable of housing up to thirty-four inmates at any one time. Each dorm had their own dayroom provided with a flat-screen television, approximately a thirty-inch screen, and enough plastic chairs for each inmate in the dorm. All televisions had cable service. Most law-abiding citizens could not afford cable or satellite service on the outside. The sound on the televisions were all muted.

The only way an inmate could hear the television was by the use of a small clear plastic battery-operated radio purchased in the local canteen. This radio was designed or especially programmed for the use of hearing the television without the television being a noise factor to others.

If an inmate was declared indigent, he would be provided a radio free of charge. Many extra radios were sold on the yards by inmates who illegally worked on radios and would sell extra parts. They obtained these extra radios from others who paid off their debts with them. Inmates who worked in the school areas would steal radio parts, such as larger capacitors, relays, and wiring, from the electric shop, enhancing better reception and a higher frequency for lucrative profit.

Every television was secured inside a locked metal container secured high on the dayroom walls. All channels were programmed on an approved television schedule; however, the inmates always figured out a way to manipulate the channel selection. Sports was the favorite program they enjoy the most other than soap operas. Their favorite soap opera was *General Hospital*. The National Football League (NFL), National Basketball Association (NBA), Major

League Baseball (MLB), soccer, college football (CFA), auto racing (NASCAR), and other sports programs were a must because they were the biggest avenue to enhance their financial status. If the administration took off a sports program on the television and substituted it for something else, you were going to have issues with the inmates. The administration refrained from this practice due to the problems it created.

Each dayroom possessed gambling rules that were strictly enforced by one particular inmate in that dorm. He monitored all the gambling activities for the head inmate in the prison who owned and secured the rights to all gambling. He would be payed a certain percentage of all the winnings from the dorm and profited from all other activity on a daily basis. If staff was fortunate enough to find out who this individual was (usually by a snitch), he would likely be placed in segregation and shipped to another prison as soon as possible.

If his inmate desired, he could transfer his gambling-controlled rights to some other inmate for temporary control or sell his right to another inmate of his choice for a lucrative amount. This was purposely done on a rotating basis to keep the staff from identifying who actually was in control of all gambling activities. It was a cat-and-mouse game; they were willing to play even though consequences were always present. Inmates were cunning but effective.

Inmates believed everything they were involved in was a game and that it was our job to catch them. They would even enter a wager with one another on which officer or staff member they could manipulate in doing something against the policy or the rules for their own selfish benefit.

Methods of gambling in prison came in many styles and forms. All inmates who gambled were always concerned about being caught due the punishment that would be imposed on them. They did not want to catch a prison charge, possibly lose their gain time, and be placed in segregation. The payoff system they used was a handwritten gambling ticket. When a wager was placed, the inmate received a very small gambling ticket, a little larger than a quarter (see pictures). The ticket would always be a carbon copy of the original because the original ticket was transferred on to the master gambling sheet, being secured by an unidentified inmate within the prison.

The master copy, if confiscated during a routine search, was not real evidence in proving whose names were on the documents. Every name on the ticket or master sheet was an alias used by inmates to protect their real identity. It was not unusual to find names such as Elvis Presley, Superman, Capone, Young Blood, Cool Breeze, Tom Hanks, Michael Jordan, Master P., and many other aliases. Some of the staff believed confiscating the main gambling sheet would eliminate the payoff on all wagers because they would not be able to verify who won. I believed, as so many other officers did, that more than one original main gambling sheet existed and there always was a backup copy. Inmates were wise and were always many steps ahead of us.

Think about this just for a minute. We were inside these fences for a short time each day, but they were there 24 hours a day, 7 days a week, and 365 days per year. Plenty of time to think and plan effective ways to avert the chance of getting caught. The inmate who did get caught with the main gambling sheet would be investigated and asked to identify the names on the list. You could bet your life that he would not say a word. Even a snitch would not do this because this would be extremely dangerous to his safety and would, for sure, get himself hurt. This was the *inmate code of silence.* He would end up catching a charge and usually doing some days in segregation. However, this was the law of the land. Inmates did not like it when their greedy gambling schemes were busted by staff, but they accepted it and continued on as if nothing occurred, only to start another gambling sheet.

Many board games were placed in the dayrooms of the dorm for recreation. These board games like Monopoly, Risk, Life, and many others were used as instruments for gambling. The dice inside these games were removed from the boxes prior to placing them in the dayroom for use. Dice were contraband and were not allowed in the prison. This, however, did not stop them. Dice would be made from toilet paper and then covered with a real hard acrylic taken from the school area. These dice were perfect and very nice (see pictures). A regular deck of Bicycle playing cards was also used as the dice.

Dominoes were especially a favorite gambling activity among themselves. These small pieces of either wood or hard plastic with dots created massive arguments and even fights. Several times, staff had to break up these games due to the amount of noise due to screaming and slamming of the dominoes down on the table. Dominoes were so popular that during several wall locker inspections, I personally would find them in their lockers and not in the dayroom as required.

Poker was a large problem. Canteen items, such as ramen noodles, potato chips, candy, toothpaste, soap, and many other items, were used as the monetary value system in the games. The biggest use of monetary payment were US postage stamps and ramen noodles. Ramen noodles were the biggest monetary system used. However, they would use anything of value to them. Staff was aware of this; however, if we did not see any of these items being transferred back and forth to one another, then they were allowed to continue to play. If any of the playing cards were marked, the colors on the cards were altered, or more cards than what was allowed in the deck, the poker game was broken up and the cards confiscated and destroyed. This happened on a regular basis. If the staff could not prove they were violating rules while playing poker, they were allowed to continue to play until the dayrooms closed for bedtime (lights out). Playing cards on the outside yard were strictly prohibited at all times. They were caught on the picnic tables many times.

Inmates would even wager on all forms of physical exercise. They would make bets on the amount of weight they could deadlift, number of bench presses on the weight pile, number of push-ups they were able to do, number of squats, and even the number of sit-ups. I observed many inmates go to medical for sick call the next morning for trying to win a bet on the weight pile and end up straining their backs or legs, hardly being able to walk. The best injury of all was their blistered pride. This was stupid and ignorant but happened all the time. They were allowed to work out on the weight piles as long as they had no medical restrictions. As staff, we could not restrict the amount of time they worked out.

It was their right, and we could not intervene unless the exercise was a cause for their safety or others. Inmates thrived at entertaining themselves with various things, but they lived to gamble every second of the day. Inmates would never stop gambling, for it was embedded deep within their minds. And to each one, it was a game they were willing to take chances even if it could be dangerous in the prison setting.

Many cell phones were found in the prison. Inmates would use these cell phones to call and make outside bets for themselves, their family, and friends. The cell phone is a dangerous device in the prison. It is used to conduct business and crime from inside the fences to the outside. The administration had realized this, and extra emphasis was placed on keeping these devices from entering the prison. They still managed to show up at times.

One could only come to this conclusion as the gambler once stated: you must know when to hold them or when to fold them.

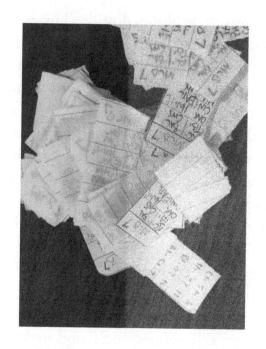

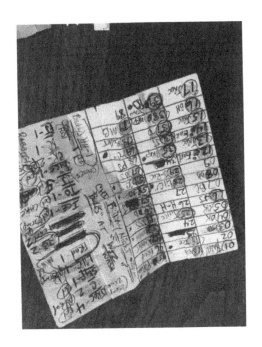

45

CHAPTER 5

The Mole in the Hole

Segregation

In our diverse society today, there seems to be a huge misconception of the term *segregation* concerning those incarcerated within the prison system. Many individuals believe this form of confinement is cruel and unusual punishment and should be abolished from the prison system.

Observing the utilization of segregation and having worked in this secured environment for over twenty-two years, I hope to shed some light at the end of the tunnel for the necessity and explanation of this custodial and security measure.

My intentions are not to convince or persuade anyone of their own personal opinion on this highly sensitive issue. For the purpose of this chapter, I will often refer to the word *segregation* as "the hole." The phrase *the hole* is one of many slang terms used by inmates as a form of communication among themselves. I will attempt to explain the types of segregation within the prison system and why segregation is a vital necessity of the security of the prison environment.

I understand why a lot of people do not approve of the term *segregation* or "the hole" because it can and does give a negative feeling that refers to a dungeon-like area set aside for punishment. This, however, is far from the truth and is so widely misunderstood.

I prefer to use the terminology *restrictive housing units*; however, segregation has been labeled the hole since the beginning of time and will never change as long as there are prisons housing incarcerated criminals.

The administration in prisons looks at "the hole" or segregation as having a negative meaning for their own political reasons and has had the term amended by their policy and prison rules, changing the use of this word. They have directed all staff and correctional personnel to use nonoffensive words, such as *special housing units* or *special holding cells*.

In prison, there are special holding cells for inmates who become violent, who have disruptive behavior and mental issues, who are pending possible transfer, and who are waiting to be paroled or released the next day. Inmates are placed in these types of confinement for administrative and security reasons. They are confined to their cell twenty-four hours per day with the exception of one hour for recreation and stretching in a designated controlled area. This includes one shower per day.

The individual cells are very small with one bed, one sink, and a toilet (see pictures). All these items are constructed of either stainless steel or metal and secured to the concrete floor and wall. The water in each individual cell is designed to be shut off by staff for all emergency situations, such as attempting to flood their cell. Each cell has a window that cannot be opened by the inmate, but they are able to look out. Ventilation in these cells are unit controlled by maintenance and not by the inmate. An outside drop-down box is secured to the front bars and doors to allow the passing of all required items, such as food, authorized clothing, medication, supplies, and writing paper for the inmate. There are a few cell doors in the segregation unit that are equipped with a solid steel door that can be shut to stop the inmates from throwing liquids, food, or feces or spitting on staff if their behavior elevates to this extreme level. The decision for shutting the solid steel door is made by the captain or lieutenant on shift. This is required for the safety and the protection of all staff and the other inmates.

The cell doors are constructed with see-through bars to ensure the correctional staff has a constant visual observation at all times. Each inmate, prior to being placed in segregation, is escorted to medical for medical clearance and for medication. If an inmate is placed in segregation for immediate security reasons or the refusal to go to medical, then the medical staff will come to the segregation unit and screen the inmate after they has been secured in their cell. This is usually a tense moment due to anger, confusion, and frustration of the inmate. It is obviously not the time or place to try to reason with an inmate on his present situation because you are removing him out of the general population, having him pack his personal belongings, inventorying his personal property, and finally conducting a fully unclothed body search on them. His ability to communicate and associate with general-populated inmates has been temporarily suspended.

While being housed inside the segregation unit, the inmate is allowed by policy certain items in their cell. These items are authorized unless they have been restricted or removed due to reasons as privilege losses for being found guilty by the unit hearing officer for violation(s) of prison rules, or he is a danger to himself or others.

- Bible / religious material, legal papers, authorized clothing, towel, and washcloth
- personal papers and pictures, personal hygiene products, and pair of shower shoes
- pair of boots or tennis shoes (all shoestrings are removed)
- canteen items
- (2) sheets, blanket, and one pillow
- one small radio with approved earbuds (except for disciplinary segregation purposes) as there are no televisions in the segregation units.

Segregated inmates are seen by medical staff on a daily basis and mental health professionals as needed. The medical staff sees and talks to each inmate on a one-on-one basis up to two times per day. Medications are issued by medical staff to ensure they have their prescribed medication on time and without delay. All medication is issued through the cell door, and the nurse monitors the inmate visually to ensure they swallow their medication they are administered and do not spit it out.

At certain times, it becomes necessary to remove an inmate from his cell once he has been segregated. This includes outside medical appointments, showering, recreation, and approved visits from their family and friends. In order to be removed from the cell, it's required by policy that the inmate be placed in full restraints, such as handcuffs attached to his waist with a black box and leg chains on both ankles. The inmate is escorted by at least two correctional officers and more if needed for his protection and safety at all times and is never left alone or out of the officer's sight. Although the inmate is in a segregated status, extreme measures are implemented and strictly enforced to ensure their safety and protection at all times. This is a mandatory requirement and is always top priority. The inmate will remain in this status until placed back into the cell, and then all the restraints are removed.

Another reason for segregation is what is referred to as "checkoff" (protective control). Some inmates who have problems paying their debts, were snitches, and for reasons unknown will request segregation; this is known as "checking off". If an inmate fails to pay his debt or has cried as a snitch, he becomes frightened and concerned for his well-being and does not want to stay in the general population until he has cleared all their obligations. This cowardly and childish pattern will get an inmate hurt, so they immediately go to the nearest officer and request immediate checkoff.

This request is, without doubt, the most sensitive issue and is handled with expedition, extreme caution, and without second thought. Remember, it is the duty of the officer to protect the inmate at all times while they are in your control. When this occurs and there is a request for protective control, the inmate is immediately removed from the area and taken to a safe location from all others. No questions are asked at this time. The inmate will be handcuffed and taken straight to a cell in segregation. His belongings will be packed and inventoried by correctional staff and not by himself.

Once this is completed, his personal items that are allowed while in protective control are transported to where the inmate is housed only by correctional staff. The inmate will have at least two or more correctional staff if necessary to personally escort him and ensure their safety at all times. Once placed in the cell, medical is called to complete his medical assessment. When this process is completed, he is afforded the same conditions as others in segregation. He is given one hour to walk or exercise. Upon feeling he is safe and the administration has taken all precautions required, the inmate can be released back into the general population with approval from the administration. Normally, this type of inmate will make the same trip back to PC in just a short time. This inmate is weak and a coward and usually ends up being bullied; however, at some point in time, his silly games will catch up to him.

According to policy (NC Department of Prisons Policy and Procedures Chapter C Section .1101), protective control is the reassignment of an inmate from the general population to confinement in a secure area to protect the inmate involved from self-injury or threat of harm by others. An inmate's request to be placed in protective control does not alone constitute grounds for reassignment. The officer in charge must evaluate all the circumstances of each case. A determination must be made that the inmate's request is legitimate and that segregation is necessary for the continued well-being of the inmate. The only purpose for protective control is the protection of the inmate when it is apparent that the inmate's life or well-being may be threatened if the subject remains in the general population.

While I was working in the prison, at no time was any inmate who requested protective control denied that I was aware of. It is the sole responsibility of the administration to provide and ensure safety at all times for every inmate. If an inmate requests protective control and gets hurt because they were denied their request, someone will be held responsible.

Removal from protective control may be considered if an inmate requests in writing to be removed from protective control status. The request will be verified, and provided no apparent constraints to the inmate' s health or personal safety can be determined, the inmate will be removed form protective control (NC Department of Prisons Policy and Procedures Chapter C Section .1102 (a) (5) and (a) (2)).

Inmates may also be segregated for seventy-two hours or less at the discretion of the officer in charge as a "cooling off" measure. No inmate may be placed in protective control for more than seventy-two hours without documented approval of the facility head or designee.

At any time, if an inmate says they are going to hurt or possibly kill themself, this inmate should be placed in segregation on what is referred to as suicide watch. Of all the reasons for segregation, this particular reason is by far is most concerning. Once the inmate has been secured on suicide watch, he will remain there and not be released by anyone other than a licensed psychiatrist or a psychologist who has given medical authorization. If determination is made that the inmate needs to be transferred to a medical hospital for further evaluation or permanent housing, this will also be made by medical professionals only.

The warden or the institutional superintendent of the prison usually does not have authority to release an inmate from suicide watch or override their medical decisions. When an inmate is placed on suicide watch for their protection, the administration has strict guidelines on this procedure. Inmates are not rational when in this frame of mind.

I have witnessed inmates attempt to cut their wrists with pieces of paint from the walls; place pencils, pens, and other objects into their own body cavities; overdose on other inmates' medication; bang their heads on the wall and floor; refuse to eat; and many more self-destructive methods. This is a serious mental condition, and they must to be placed in a safe and secured environment. Although this may seem cruel, the prison system is there to protect them at all costs. When an inmate is placed on suicide watch, several precautions are used for their own protection and safety. The inmate is placed into a special cell with a bed with no mattress or pillow.

They have no sheets and no property or anything. The inmate will be completely stripped nude with no clothing and covered with only a green blanket that cannot be torn or tied.

This is the only item he has to cover himself. This blanket is referred to as the turtle blanket by all inmates. Inside each cell, their toilet seat can be locked, and the water can be shut off. All their meals are served on Styrofoam plates. They're given no silverware or eating utensils and have to eat with their hands only. This seems cruel but is necessary and effective and keeps them from hurting or taking their own life.

The use of segregation is not taken lightly. It requires extra staff and manpower. One staff member is assigned to do nothing but monitor him every second of the day. All his movements, awake or asleep, are recorded on a report every fifteen minutes. At no time do you want an inmate to take his life while in prison and especially while he is being housed in "suicide watch." I do not believe there is a good enough excuse or explanation for this happening, although it does. There is no reason an inmate should kill themselves in segregation unless the staff is incompetent and not doing their job. Just recently, there was news of a high-profile inmate who managed to die. Whether he (Jeffrey Epstein) killed himself or was killed, there is no excuse. Staff must be accountable. If an inmate wants to hurt himself bad enough, he will try and sometimes, unfortunately, does succeed. I vividly remember one particular inmate while in segregation hung himself with their own bedsheet, but this occurred only one time in my tenure as a correctional officer. (This particular inmate was not on suicide watch). I attribute this sole incident to the strict rules and guidelines set forth by the administration and the policies on the handling of these type of inmates.

Inmates often refer to the hole as a place for their well-needed vacation. Why not? They are given individual personal attention, and they take full advantage at all times. Segregation caters to the inmate. These inmates are waited on hand and foot by the staff.

They have all three (3) meals brought and served to them by staff and do not have to go to the dining facility. Their clothing change, library call, canteen (commissary), medications, and newspaper are all completed by staff. They just lay in their beds, do push-ups in their cell, listen to music, read books, sing and rap, and get plenty of rest and sleep. Some inmates go to segregation only because they want and need a break from the normal routine of being incarcerated and dealing with others in the general population. There is a need for the hole, segregation, or whatever you prefer to call it in the penitentiary system. Inmates, although incarcerated, must be held accountable for all their actions, and as for the correctional staff, they need this important control measure to protect them and others at all times. Some inmates love the hole so much they are often labeled as "the mole in the hole" by other inmates.

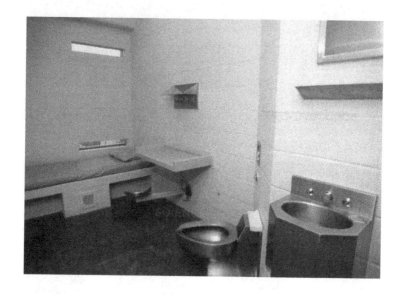

CHAPTER 6

The Dirty Officer
The Inmates' and the Convicts' Best Friend

There is a vast difference in the true definition of an *inmate* and a *convict*. Both terms are used in defining an individual who is incarcerated in most penitentiaries or jail systems. An inmate normally will not have been in these systems but for a short period and does not fully comprehend the devious thought patterns or behaviors of a true convict. On the other hand, a convict has been in the system for many years and has been given a lifetime before he gets out if they ever get released. They are the king of deception within the system. Both of these individuals are cunning and willing to do anything to get over on the system. The convict is wiser and more heinous than the ordinary inmate and understands all the prison rules, policies, and the law better than most of the staff. They make it their top priority to be one step ahead of everyone and everything at all times no matter the cost, for they have nothing to lose. A convict will always tell you, "I am not an inmate," every opportunity he gets. Both of these individuals are a challenge

GLEN R. REED JR.

to the administration and staff on a daily basis; however, when dealing with a convict, you better be on your toes at all times, or you could find yourself caught in a situation that causes you problems, your reputation, your job, and in some cases, your own family.

Many inmates and convicts thrive on the idea of buttering up to an officer for the sole purpose of their own benefit. I have witnessed this situation many times, and the end results are always devastating. One example is where an inmate, while in prison and through his deceitfulness, wiggled his way into the personal life of a female prison chaplain. After convincing her that he needed her help, she fell into his trap and eventually ended up giving him her pantyhose.

Why did he want her pantyhose? He wanted control over her for his own devious and selfish reasons. He could care less about her pantyhose. The conclusion of his relentless pressure resulted in her losing her job. The inmate loses nothing but the possibly of a few days in segregation and usually ends up cutting a plea bargain for turning the individual into the administration. Many officers have been caught in these baited traps. I personally had no use for the "dirty officer" (a coward in uniform). These officers are not worthy to wear the correctional uniform and should have always been prosecuted to the full extent of the law. However, the administration, due to the high cost and headache of going to court, would rather just walk them out of the prison gate and be finished with them.

The seriousness of being a dirty officer or staff is they are subjecting good professional officers and staff to potential danger in their performance of duty on a daily basis. They do not care, or they would not be dirty.

One individual who worked in the maintenance section was dealing with a particular inmate who convinced him to bring marijuana into the prison. This staff member would obtain the amount of contraband the inmate requested and sneak it into the prison. In return, the inmate would make all the necessary arrangements to have his friend or family member on the outside place the money the dirty staff member was being paid into a post office box in a designated post office outside. Eventually, after doing this for some time, the inmate turned him over to the administration probably because he wanted to increase the amount of contraband, or he was done using him for his deviant purpose. Once an inmate or convict gets their claws in a dirty officer, they will demand more and more of them, and when they refuse, the inmate or convict will roll over on them and find another dirty officer to replace their needs and wants.

Inmates will use any individual in authority to enhance their financial status and selfish reasons. They might respect you and not bother you, but if you let your guard down, they will pounce on you like a vulture looking for their next meal. Of all the incredible and nasty situations they employ, the one that is most disgusting is using dirty staff for their sexual favors. One night after all the yards had closed and all the inmates were inside their respective dorms, the yard officer went to the back side of this dorm for his normal security check. As he peeked into the window of the dormitory, he observed a female officer on her knees under the table performing oral sex on an inmate. She was quickly escorted out of the prison, being terminated from her job, and the inmate in question was placed in segregation. This particular officer was married—a total disgrace to herself, her husband, her friends, and her family. This is far beyond one's imagination because this type of behavior is so filthy, not to mention all the diseases associated with acts of this nature. Not only did this officer bring discredit upon herself, she possibly could be taking home a serious disease outside the confines of the prison to her family, friends, and the public.

Again, she should have been charged and prosecuted for a sexual crime but was only terminated from her job and escorted out of the prison. The best policy in dealing with these criminal minds is not to give them anything, not even the time of day. Inmates are inquisitive by nature. They start with little items that seem so minor and innocent, but it is the foundation to their overall purpose and plan in obtaining something from you. Examples of questions they ask are, "Are you married?" "How many children do you have?" "What kind of vehicle do you prefer?" "Where do you live?" "What kind of sports do you watch on television?" and "What is your favorite football team?" These seem very innocent questions, but they don't bother to ask them because they are friendly or trying to be kind. They desire to know your likes and dislikes for their devious scheme to haul you into their claws and eventually use them to squeeze you into their own selfish plan. An inmate and especially a convict will start with a very small and inadequate favor. They may ask you for something like,

"My watchband is broken, and I need a small inexpensive one to hold me over until I can afford a new one. Would you mind and bring me another one, and by the way, it does not have to be new or even match my broken one." The dirty officer, believing this and not asking much, brings them a watchband. A few weeks later, he might approach him again and need a pack of cigarettes and then batteries for his radio.

Soon it might be pornography pictures and illicit magazines. Eventually, the dirty officer being drawn into the inmate's grasp is told and not asked to bring in dangerous contraband, such as drugs, weapons, cell phones, and even alcohol. Small bottles of alcohol from a liquor store have been found in the prison during searches and unit shakedowns.

Eventually the inmate and convict go in for the kill on their objective or overall plan. If the dirty officer refuses, he is threatened with his job by the inmate or convict. The dirty officer will either give them what they want or never return to work again, forfeiting their job in fear of retaliation. I saw many not return to work obviously for these reasons.

Over the years, many officers have been caught in what they describe as true love. This is not love but merely an infatuation. How an individual in prison could support a spouse or their children doesn't make good sense when all they really care about is doing illegal and unethical practices to support their own greed and lust. An inmate will treat an officer, male or female, with the upmost respect with false promises of giving them the world. What's so disgusting about these incredible lies is the dirty officer ends up believing them and becomes so emotionally involved, sometimes ending up having a physical affair inside the very fences of the place they work. I have known a few officers who traveled down this muddy road.

The inmate talk is sweet to a deaf ear and is very decisive. After being caught by the administration, I have known the dirty officer to marry the same inmate or convict after they lose their job, respect, and dignity. They are on the outside, and their so-called lover is still doing time on the inside. How ridiculous. I had a fellow officer who worked in the prison who got caught up in having an inmate draw a simple picture of his family member. He ended up being unemployed and looking for another job in just a few weeks.

Others lost their job for simple things like breaking a large currency bill into smaller denominations, becoming a banker in prison. At that time, a five-dollar bill was the largest allowed in the prison.

Why would one go to all the headache of doing things for inmates and convicts? The answer is simple. They are "dirty."

They need to be weeded out of this type of employment, and the administration does their best just to do that. This overall type of behavior for profit or favor from a dirty officer can cause major issues within the prison, thus making the good officer more acceptable to being hurt and even maimed for life.

The old saying "If you play with fire, you will get burned" is the overall results of the dirty correctional officer.

It is a crying shame that this type of behavior exists within the prison but is also a fact of life. As I said before, they are not worthy of wearing the uniform of the correctional officer. They should be doing time also. The administration must never deviate from exposing and removing the dirty correctional officer and should always punish them with the full extent of the law no matter the cost.

Always separate the "tares amongst the wheat."

CHAPTER 7

Boys with Deadly Toys
Weapons of Self-Destruction

Boys will be boys due to the circumstances surrounding their daily lives, and this can be no more evident than inside the walls and fences of the penitentiary. This internal mechanism of being a man is normal; however, when these internal desires no longer fit into the norm of society or the prison, they can become very dangerous and even deadly. This must be dealt with immediately.

Inmates love their homemade weapons and will go the extra mile to ensure they possess exactly what they need or want in order to complete these weapons of self-destruction no matter the damaging results to themselves, their fellow inmates, or others who work in the prison setting.

Within these razor wire fences, one can only imagine the amount of homemade deadly weapons that are produced on a daily basis by these criminal minds in order to protect themselves and create unnecessary havoc to others.

The amount of time and effort needed to prepare and obtain materials for these weapons are not a factor, for they have all the time they need and have nothing else to do. They want the best materials they can obtain and put great effort and pride in the final outcome of each and every weapon made. Most of these weapons are used for battering or sold to other inmates within the prison for profit. This is a real concern for the correctional staff due to the safety of one another and the entire population within the prison.

These criminal minds make these insane deadly weapons in such a matter that it will make the ordinary individual ponder on how in the world they got these ideas while being incarcerated in a secured and guarded environment. This is precisely why most of them are there. They are not in prison for chopping down a cherry tree. If you have ever seen the television series with Richard Dean who played MacGyver and his Swiss pocketknife, you can get some idea of the caliber of ingenuity inmates possess.

During my tenure, I observed a homemade knife that you would think was purchased on the street. This particular knife was the knife above all knives. It was large and had been made from a bastard file out in the maintenance area. The knife was clean as stainless steel with a perfect design that even had a fuller in the blade. The edge was extremely razor-sharp and had a very fine point.

The handle on the knife was unbelievably carved from a bone most likely out of the dining facility. The carvings were unique and had very precise designs that only an artist could have done. The handle was so shiny you would think it was factory made. This particular weapon was not made overnight. It took many months and even possibly a few years to make.

This knife was made with the purpose to hurt and even kill someone. The brilliance of this weapon, although very unique, was just one of many other weapons made with the same end results from items of everyday use by the inmate. One easy-to-obtain item is the ordinary plastic toothbrush. The toothbrush is made available for every inmate, and in most cases, they possessed two or three at one time. In the prison, the most common weapon made from a tooth-brush was referred to as a *shank* or other terms such as a *poker* or a *shiv*. The ordinary plastic toothbrush sharpened at the end with a fine point can be used on an individual, causing very serious injury and even death. The brush end of the toothbrush was usually wrapped with paper, cloth, and tape, creating a handle for this weapon. It was very primitive but just as effective as a knife bought in a store today. Several toothbrushes combined with other materials have been made into a small bow and arrow (see picture).

They even made their own arrows. One of the weapons made with a toothbrush or an ink pen is the one referred to as a "double nickle" or, in the urban language, the "Gillette bayonet." The pen or the toothbrush is modified with two disposable razor blades melted on both sides. One sweep across the face or any part of the body usually leaves two long deep cuts, causing a large permanent scar, disfiguring the individual for life. Another weapon is usually a whip-type weapon with razor blades attached to several small ropes or string and swung at an individual, creating large cuts wherever the razor blades come in contact with the body.

The maintenance area of the prison is a supply store for these weapons. When inmates work in this area, contraband will be removed and spread into the prison no matter the amount of security. Inmates are *thieves of all thieves*. They have access to all tools, such as screwdrivers, wrenches, hammers, and many other dangerous items, and when placed in the wrong hands, it is not conceivable that some are stolen or have been reported lost. The correctional officer and the administration enforce extensive policies and procedures on the handling of all materials and tools; however, you cannot control the inevitable. Apples or oranges and even a simple hamburger end up missing out of the dining facility and found in an inmate's wall locker; what makes one think you can keep materials from them for making weapons? You are only naive and fooling yourself.

Chocolate is sweet to the tooth, and everyone loves it, including inmates. Chocolate in candy bars is not always sweet but can become bitterly dangerous. Although during my tenure as a correctional officer I never observed this type of incident, it does happen. Inmates will melt the chocolate in a container to where it becomes a hot chocolate liquid. If the chocolate is thrown on your face, arms, or other parts of the body, it sticks and causes major burns.

These are not simple burns but deep burns that usually require special medical attention. The handles on regular mop buckets were removed because these handles, when sharpened, make a highly effective weapon with little effort.

There are many other types of weapons, such as a padlock in a sock, spears, clubs, steel knuckles, and even AAA batteries that can be taped together and thrown at someone. As long as there are individuals incarcerated, there will be weapons of self-destruction within the prison. Inmates in prison become institutionalized and dangerous to themselves and others and will always have their own "weapons of self-destruction."

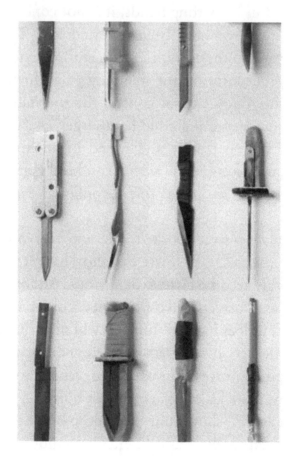

PRISON MADE SHIVS AND KNIVES

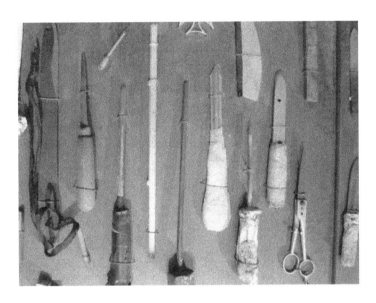

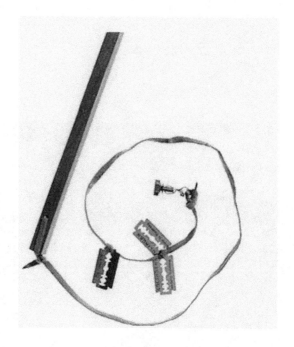

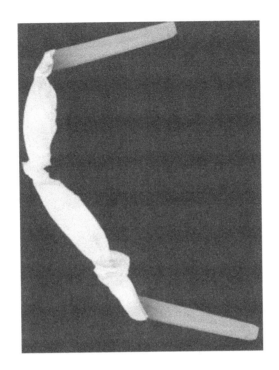

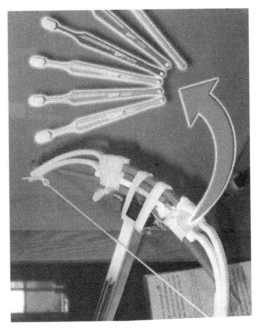

73

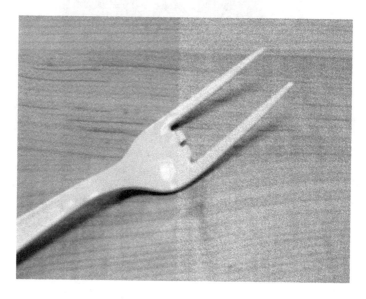

CHAPTER 8

Tit for Tat
The Ink Pusher

Tit for tat is a word meaning "the infliction of an injury or insult in return for one that has suffered." This fits the definition for inmates in prison; however, in this chapter, I will describe this term in a different scope for another purpose of the prison environment. In the prison, there is so much talent that it makes one think why they are incarcerated. In the prison, you have artists who can draw and paint the best pictures you will ever see or purchase. Among these artists is the notorious "ink pusher". This highly talented inmate is the *tattoo artist*. This inmate is extremely respected and possesses an extremely large, lucrative business. The word *tattoo* is often referred to as tat by the inmates. To have been tattooed in prison is referred to as have been "dotted."

There are several of these individuals who take a lot of pride in their ink work and will do anything to be the best there is. Most of your tattoos in prison are done in black-and-white ink, but there are some inked in color. I have seen the both of them on a daily basis. These inmates will do just about anything to ensure they possess the necessary and the best tattoo equipment there is available to them in the prison.

As far as tattoo equipment, they made their own tattoo guns, needles, ink, and all other items needed to get the job done. Most tattoo guns were very small and primitive but as effective as the ones purchased on the outside economy. Their needles for these guns were effective, and some were even made from the string of a guitar, paper clips, and stolen needles from the medical section. It is amazing to see a needle made out of the string of a guitar. In some way, they managed to heat and split this instrument's string and ensure it is effective. Tattoo guns are made with a small motor obtained from the maintenance section, electrical school, and contraband from the outside.

Most items are from the dirty staff member bringing them into the prison as illegal contraband. The base of these guns will usually be a small ink pen, spoon, pencil, and the most favorite, the small Sharpie marker. However, they would use whatever they can get their hands on. They produce their own ink in various ways. They burn paper, grind up pencil lead, add oil, then heat up and use it. One particular way that was prevalent was a regular can of Kiwi shoe polish. The inmate would fill this with baby oil. They put a small hole in the top of the can, and a wick of some type is inserted.

The oil is used to burn the wick. The soot is scraped off the can and patted to remove any excess oil. This is added to toothpaste or oils, and they have their ink. This is unsanitary and can cause a lot of infection.

Tattooing in some cases caused the spread of HIV, AIDS, hepatitis B and C, and many other diseases. Their favorite ink is from the new gel pens found on the market today. The ink is already in a plastic tube filter and comes in many selected colors. These were not sold in the canteen. They get these from the dirty staff member.

The tattoo is a symbolic way of life in the prison.

The tattoos tell the story of their life, their crime, and how long they are in prison. The tattoo is used to display the gang lifestyle that they belong to in society. This no more evident than in Russian prisons. Inmates will tattoo themselves anywhere on their bodies, including under their eyelids, inside their lips, and under their armpits. They even tattoo areas on their bodies that the average person would cringe or regurgitate just to think about.

Inmates that are validated as true gang members are placed into a special category known as STG (special threat groups). These individuals that are validated as STG are usually covered with tattoos displaying their unique individual gang affiliations.

Inside the normal prison environment, gangs try to control certain areas for their own use. This creates vast problems for the correctional officer and between other gang affiliations and is an ongoing problem that is dealt with immediately when this occurs or has been identified. Every gang member has his leader or person that is the strongest mentally with more seniority and is considered to be in full control at all times, the head of his pecking order. This individual normally calls the shots and is responsible for the actions of members under his control.

Early identification of these groups is essential to the overall safety of all in the prison and society.

Tattoos play a large part in this identification process. All officers are trained on a yearly basis on gangs, their tattooing of their leaders, and all activities not only in the prison environment but also in society itself.

This training is very extensive due to the seriousness of gangs today. By mere definition, a prison gang is an inmate organization that has a corporate entity, that exists into perpetuity, and whose membership is restrictive, mutually exclusive, and requires a lifetime commitment.

In prison, you can identify gang members by their own distinctive gang-related tattoos. Some of these gangs were the following:

La Eme or the Mexican Mafia MS-13
Dead Man Incorporated
Aryan Brotherhood
Asian Boys
Juggalos Sureno
Nuestra Familia
Nazi Lowriders
Outlaws
Bloods
Latin Kings
Crips
5 Percenters
Texas Syndicate
Netas: Puerto Rican
The Black Guerilla Family

Folk Nation
DC Blacks
Conservative Vice Lords
Public Enemy No. 1
Dirty White Boys
KKK
Hells Angels
Moorish Nation
Warlocks
Southside Locos

These are just a few gang members housed in our prisons. There are many others. All identified by their tattoos; the way they wear their shoes, hats, and clothing; and their gang signs.

Inmates seem to like certain tattoos. These seem to be their favorite ones. Most inmates will have one of these simple tattoos on their body. They normally were a clock or watch (no hands), dollar sign (money), "Momma Tried," devil with horns, "In God We Trust" and "Born to Raise Hell," and symbols with the use of numbers.

Most prison tattoos have a certain meaning and display the gang they are affiliated with. Here are a few examples.

- *1488.* This number is found on white supremacist and Nazi inmates. They will rotate these numbers to try to confuse staff. They have this often placed on their foreheads. The number 14 represents fourteen words which were quoted by Nazi David Lane: "We must secure the existence of our people and a future for white children." The number 88 is for the 8th letter of the alphabet written twice. HH represents Heil Hitler. These symbols and letters are found on all parts of the body.

- *A.C.A.B.* This tattoo often refers to "All cops are bastards" and "Always carry a Bible." Found normally on their knuckles or back.
- *Playing cards.* The inmate likes to gamble. One card suite on each finger as a spade, diamond, heart, and clubs.
- *MS 13.* Seen on inmates as *MS* and *13* or combined. This is the symbol of the Mara Salvatrucha gang from El Salvador. The gang was started in California. This is found on all parts of the body and are highly visible.
- *Norento.* This represents the Nuestra Familia gang, which is associated with Hispanic gangs. Their tattoos include the word *Norento*, a *sumbrero* symbol, the letter *N*, and the number 14, which is the 14th letter of the alphabet. They identify themselves with red bandannas and deal in narcotics, drugs, and smuggling.
- *La Eme.* Or the letter *M* is the symbol of the Mexican mafia. They are one of the largest and most ruthless gangs in our prisons in the US. They are affiliated with the Aryan Brotherhood, and both dislike the Nuestra Familia. The gang was not started in Mexico; however, most members were Mexican Americans who were incarcerated in US

prisons. La Eme is a Sureno gang affiliated with Hispanic gangs in California.

- *Aryan Brotherhood.* This particular prison gang has a large variety of tattoos. The gang makes up approximately 1 to 2 percent of the inmate population. They have tattoo symbols such as SS bolts, AB, Nazi symbols, and the swastika.

- *Clock with no hands.* This has the meaning of doing time, and of great extent and tattooed on their wrist with straps like a real wristwatch. The clock comes in a few forms, such as a wall clock or grandfather clock without hands. Not all clock tattoos are tied to prison, usually the ones with missing hands.

- *Five dots.* This represents time done in prison. Known as the quincunx, the four dots on the outside represent four walls, and the fifth dot on the inside the prisoner. This is usually found on the hands between the thumb and forefinger. The five dots on other parts of the body have a different meaning as having association with the People Nation gang.

- *Five-pointed star (crown).* This symbol is of the Latin Kings gang. This is one of the largest Hispanic gangs in the US out of Chicago. The crown will often be accompanied by the letters *ALKN*, which refers to the Almighty Latin Kings Nation. The five points on the crown are due to the Latin Kings being an affiliate of the People Nation gang, which is represented by the number 5. This gang has a large presence in both the prison and the outside. The crown can have colors with hidden meanings.

- *The cobweb.* These tattoos represent a lengthy term in prison. It is associated with spiders trapping their prey or criminals trapped behind bars. This is found mostly on the elbow because you have been sitting around so long that a spider has made a web on you. This can also be seen on the neck.
- *Cross on the chest.* This particular tattoo symbolizes a "prince of thieves." This marking is found a lot in Russian prisons. This is also used for religious reasons.
- <u>*Teardrop*</u>. This is the most recognized prison tattoo. The meaning for this tattoo is based on the area you are from. The tattoo can mean a long sentence or that you as the wearer have committed murder. If the tattoo is not completely colored inside, you have attempted murder. The teardrop has been made popular by rappers and other celebrities. Those who are new inmates behind bars with a teardrop have a lot of enemies.

One afternoon, as we were conducting a unit shakedown, I noticed an inmate that had a red outline on the back of his white undershirt. Upon having him remove his shirt, it was discovered on his back a fresh tattoo of some Hispanic meaning. It was a large tattoo that covered 50 percent of his back, still red, raw, and bleeding. The red on his shirt was his blood coming through the shirt. This particular tattoo was a masterpiece well inked with many colors. The Virgin Mary was the main design of the tattoo. It was outlined with beautiful flowers, trees, and a scenic view of mountains and people in the background. He admitted getting the tattoo over the past three days and, of course, would not tell on the tattoo artist. This did not matter to him because his tattoo was complete, and after a few days in segregation, he would be back out in the general population displaying his beautiful new tattoo among the other inmates. A picture by camera of his new tattoo was taken by the STG officer and entered into his prison record for future reference. When I asked him what his tattoo symbolized and who was the tattoo artist, he smiled and just said, "It looks good."

Many times, tattoo guns were found in the prison.

Although these were confiscated and destroyed by the administration, you can bet another one was being made somewhere right under our noses. As long as there are prisoners in prison, there will always be the tattoos. I have added a few pictures to this chapter displaying some of the tattoos you find on an inmate, and as you will see, the tattoo tells their story and their ranking structure within the gang they are associated with. For this is their purpose in life behind these fences, and this is "tit for tat."

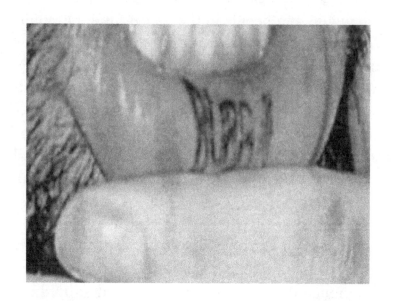

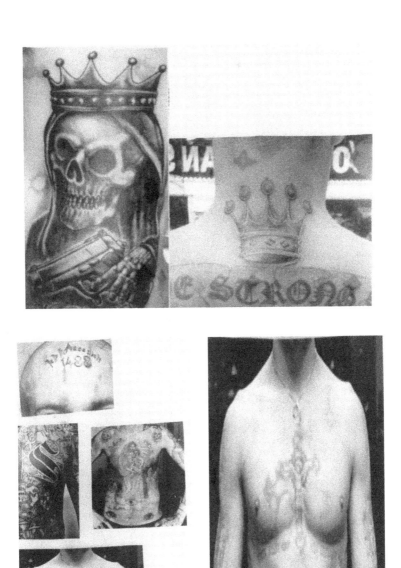

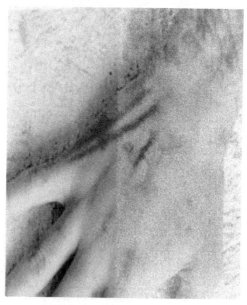

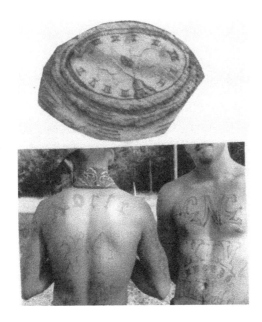

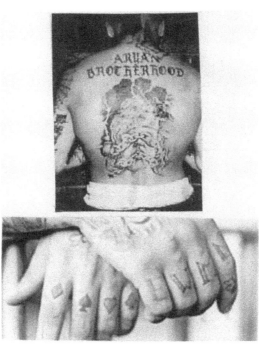

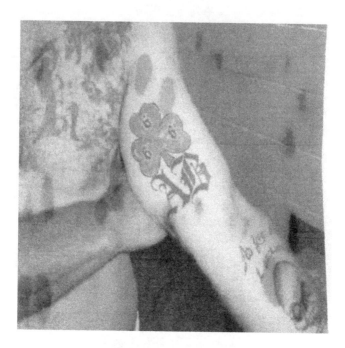

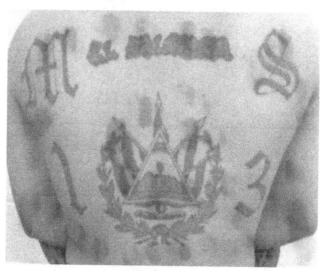

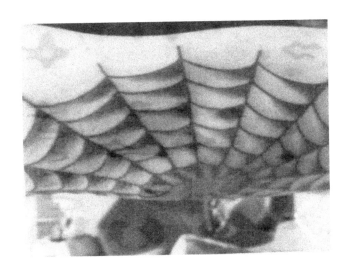

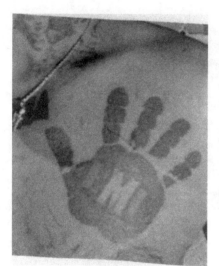

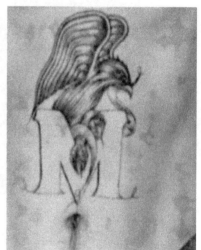

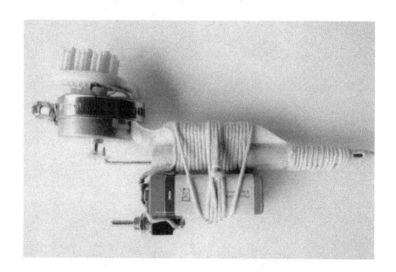

CHAPTER 9

Choose This Day Whom You Will Serve

Deep within every human being, there is the soul, and there comes a time in each of our lives when we come to the realization that there is a greater force of power other than man. This power is known as God.

Every human being believes in something; that is why I believe there is no such thing as a *true atheist*. We all believe in something even if it is our *own self*. This is true for all mankind even for the meanest, cruelest, and most ruthless individuals in our penitentiaries today.

Every inmate I have ever encountered or had a conversation with believed there is this a power above mankind, with the exception of a few. Even the nonbelieving inmate, although he says he does not believe in any form of deity, still reads and clings to his own bible or religious material while being incarcerated. Every inmate is religious in the sense of the word.

There are several types of beliefs in prison as there is in society. Some are recognized by society today, and some are not. This is evident by the prison administration authorizing most types of worship within the confines of the prison. Some prisons have well-built chapels (churches) within the area of the prison for the incarcerated to meet and exercise their religious belief. In prison, just about every inmate attaches himself to a religious entity of some type, form, or fashion. Most inmates become religious.

The prison I was associated with had a nice building referred to as the chapel. The chapel had pews, chairs, piano, musical instruments, many Bibles, and other religious materials. The prison had its own chorus made up of inmates from all different cultures, backgrounds, and faith. This caused some contention and disagreement among themselves as to who was allowed to be in the chorus and who was not. Some of the inmates did not want an inmate who was homosexual on the choir. Issues always worked out, and they would sing their hearts out during each scheduled service.

Most prisons had an established chaplain on the staff. His or her background was not always from the same denomination, so many changes occurred over periods of time. The chaplain I remember at the time was a Baptist chaplain. He was very effective with all the inmates; however, when a certain group of inmates from another faith wanted the cross removed from the wall in the chapel, this caused a lot of problems. Because of his stand for his belief, it was evident this was not going to happen while he was assigned as the chaplain.

The administration seemed to believe it was all right to remove the cross and place it back on the wall only for the use of the Protestant faith services. Due to his convictions and strong belief, he resigned as the chaplain because of this issue, and a new chaplain was brought in. I admired his strong convictions.

Although this might seem minor, I personally believe he was right for taking a stand for his belief. We had chaplains from all beliefs and various backgrounds.

One chaplain smoked a pipe and often used excessive profanity. A chaplain is one that ministers to all faiths; however, they are required by their own belief and faith to preach and teach what they were called to do, not what the administration or the prison department desires. It eventually resulted in there being no assigned chaplain. The administration assigned a nonqualified staff member to perform the duties of the chaplain. This particular individual was not called by God or ordained by a denomination. He was a case manager for the inmates.

The administration is governed by policies and procedures and our Constitution ensuring all inmates are given their right to pray and worship. I believe every inmate had that opportunity, but different groups were allowed more privileges than others because the administration not wanting any religious groups creating public and or political issues within the prison. The administration tried to please all inmates on their religious practices and preferences; however, they bent over backward for some groups and not for other groups. Some groups were afforded special feasts and meals on special occasions, have certain food fed to them at certain times of the day for an established period, go on approved extended times for prayer, and were fed at certain times. These groups were for the most part not of the Protestant faith.

After the authorized and sanctioned religious period, they were authorized to end their special program with a feast of celebration. Most of the food would be prepared by the dining facility in the prison, and some special food items were authorized to be brought into the prison from an outside source. Again, this was not afforded to every religious group. For example, no special food or privileges were given for those who celebrated Easter, this being one of the biggest religious holidays of the year. Another example was the Native American religion.

The prison was a totally smoke-free environment. Smoking or tobacco products of all forms or fashion were considered contraband and were confiscated if found. If you were of the Native American faith, you were authorized to have in your possession a "sacred box." This sacred box contained different types of sacred herbs, kinnikinnick, white sage, certain grass, cedar for smudging pots, certain feathers, beads, and even an authorized Native American pipe for their ceremonial smoking. At certain designated times set by the administration, a large circle was placed on the yard, and during this ceremony, these inmates would light up and pass the pipe around to one another. This was controlled by correctional staff. However, these inmates were not allowed outside of the circle. The sacred box was authorized to be stored in their own personal wall lockers. The sacred box was not allowed to be touched by any correctional officer or staff due to their religious belief. If it were to be inspected, the inmate owning the sacred box would remove the items in front of you to observe and inspect but not for you to physically touch. When completed, the items were placed back into their box by the inmate. No other religious groups could smoke for any reason.

The policy is very clear and states, "Tobacco paraphernalia includes rolling papers, pipes or other products used to smoke, inhale or ingest tobacco products. This does not include American Indian Ceremonial pipes which may remain in the possession of the inmate" (NC DPS Policy and Procedures, SECTION .2500, Chapter F).

This policy, however written, caters to a special religious group and has favoritism and racial discrimination written all over it. There is no way around it. One of the other religious groups was allowed to wear large green, yellow, and red knitted headgear to cover their hair. This is indicative of granting some religious groups more privilege's than others. An inmate was not allowed to wear a cross around their neck if they were of the Christian faith.

This is unjust and not fair.

Inmates were allowed in most cases to change their religious affiliation upon request. The inmate would submit a request in writing through their perspective case manager, and the decision, once made, was returned to them upon approval or disapproval. Inmates would change their religious preference for the sole purpose of receiving the special benefits and special religious dietary meals they could not obtain from their present religious affiliation.

Inmates used religion as a crutch to obtain what they desired and belong to some other group for their own self-satisfaction and protection. They used this avenue to obtain special clothing and religious materials. The inmate population has several different religious groups, such as Baptist, Pentecostal, Mormon, Unitarian, Rastafarian, Muslim, Nation of Islam, Moorish Science Temple, Jehovah's Witness, Jewish, Catholic, Buddhist, Hindu, and many more, not to leave out witchcraft, such groups like the Wiccans. The Wiccans used *The Book of Shadows* for their bible. This book contained religious text and instructions for magical rituals found within the neo-pagan religion and many other pagan groups. I run into problems while conducting searches where the inmate had refused to allow me to touch this book.

The administration would have the inmate open the book in front of me, and I was visually able to inspect it. I really did not want to touch it per se, but the Holy Bible was not of limits to any type of inspection or search. Again, this is another loophole for the inmate to change to his religion for deceptive and selfish reasons.

Outside religious groups were authorized to enter the prison on a certain time schedule in the evenings and on Sundays to hold their Bible study groups with the inmates. This practice seemed to help with problems of the inmates trying to establish their own Bible studies. These religious groups were approved by the administration and were open to all inmates who wanted to attend their study group.

Religion plays a big role in the prison environment.

Not everyone believes the same religious doctrine; however, this seems to keep down the friction among the different cultures and allows the inmate to freely worship in his own way and style. In the prison, there are many different personalities and backgrounds, and inmates use religion as a benefit at all times. "Choose this day whom you will serve."

CHAPTER 10

Smokeless and Cashless

"The love of money is the root of all evil." There is nothing wrong with having money; however, the love of money can and will usually destroy you. In the penitentiary, the inmate has an extreme love for money. It's an avid desire so evil that entices their greed to the point that they will do anything in order to fill their pockets. It has also been said, "Poverty breeds violence, not safety."

Inmates were paid weekly in cash by the unit accounting clerk until the prison became cashless. Normal pay call was early in the morning prior to the breakfast meal being fed. The accounting officer would have each inmate in the dorm sign for their weekly pay. These payments were made in cash with no increment larger than a five-dollar bill. Payroll was made on a Tuesday basis for working assigned jobs within the prison. Jobs with a monetary payment to the inmate were the meat plant operator, soap plant operator, cooks, dorm and yard janitors, maintenance workers, and the lavish job of road squad (road workers). There were other jobs. This was called incentive pay. The average inmate salary was forty cents per day at approximately two dollars and eighty cents per week. Some jobs paid one dollar per day. The money disbursed came out of the financial office. Inmates received a weekly computer-generated printout of the balance in their personal account.

The amount of money in their account was their money, but they were only authorized to draw out forty dollars per week. If they possessed any amount above the authorized forty dollars on their possession at any one time, the inmate would be in violation of excessive funds. The extra money above the forty dollars would be confiscated and returned to the unit inmate morale fund, and the inmate would be charged for possessing funds above the authorized amount.

Many times, during searches and normal routine pat-down searches, inmates were found to possess greater amounts of money on them than the authorized forty dollars. At times, they were found to possess amounts over a hundred dollars in their possession. This was because they collected from other inmates for payments of debts, gambling, and other illegal activities. It was never unusual to find an inmate holding larger amounts of money.

One day, a brown paper bag found on the compound containing over $900. This bag was found on the roof of a dormitory. This was the main pot of money used for the payoff on an NFL football gambling pool. Some inmates had substantial amounts of money but would spread their wealth over the prison population with other inmates who were indigent or did not get a drawl that week to hold for them. They would receive a small payment for holding these funds. But it was not theirs.

The commissary or canteen referred to by the inmate was where they purchased personal items, radios, and food they desired or used for trading purposes. It never made sense when accounting inventoried the canteens and discovered more money was being spent in the canteens than was disbursed on the compound for payroll that week. Money was everywhere at any given time and especially during sports, such as the National Football League (NFL), National Basketball Association (NBA), NASCAR, and many collegiate sports.

Weekly payments for their jobs were not the only avenue for them to obtain money placed into their personal accounts. An inmate received money from their family members, local churches, friends, and other sources. Mail call was especially interesting because all these activities could send a money order in various amounts to the inmate, and the money was then placed into their personal account. The mail room would open the letter, then remove the money order and process it. Of all the devious but extremely effective scams, one was where the inmate would contact an individual from the opposite sex on the outside and become their pen pal.

A lot of these pen pals became "paper love affairs," with the individual sending the inmate money orders every week or so. The inmate convinced these pen pals that they were poor, indigent, and needed financial help in order to survive while behind bars. Just think for a moment, if an inmate is receiving funds from ten to twenty pen pals, their personal account becomes very lucrative. Some inmates' accounts were larger than those of law-abiding citizens working hard jobs in society. This scam has evolved into the pen pal becoming so infatuated with the inmate's paper-loving relationship that some end up getting married with their pen pal. However, the inmate continues to receive money orders from all other pen pals on their shifty scam game. I guess all's fair in love and war!

The rules were recently changed effective February 5, 2019, on a letterhead from the director of prisons stating that the department wanted to ensure that all inmates resided in its facilities without the fear of strong arming and/or undue influence to commit an illicit act of monetary gain. Prisons will restrict all depositors into the trust fund accounts to only those listed as approved visitors of the inmate. The memo was clear that all funds still must go through and be processed through JPay (Memo NC DPS, 2019). This sounds great, but in due time, the inmate will eventually find a way to bypass this rule and continue to pad their pockets. Again, it is just a matter of time.

The Department of Corrections realized that having cash within the prison caused many problems for them and the prison administrators. Some prisons had already changed to what is referred as cashless camps.

What is JPay? This is an organization that is a privately held corrections-related service provider with its headquarters based in Miramar, Florida. The company contracts with state department of corrections (DOC), county jails, and private federal prisons to provide technologies and services, including money transfer, email, video visitation, parole, and probation payments to 1.5 million inmates through-out at least thirty-five states. All funds sent to an inmate must be sent through this program. The web address is JPay.com.

One must go to the home page, and there you will be directed on how to transfer money and other services to an inmate. This system has been under scrutiny, and possible lawsuits were filed against them.

Due to the prison being cashless, the administration has set up a system using a prison identification card assigned to each inmate. These cards had their prison picture and their prison ID number on each inmate card. The card was computer and photo generated. All transactions were done by the use of this card for all activities. No more buying something with cash. Wrong again! This made the use of money invalid, but still some cash managed to be found. The inmates just found another effective way to substitute the use of money by creating their own currency system, the US postage stamp. Every inmate was authorized a certain amount of stamps in their possession at one given time. I believe it was twenty-five at one time if my memory serves me right. But many were caught with excessive amounts above the authorized limit. These excess stamps were confiscated as unauthorized contraband, and the inmate could be charged for an unauthorized number of stamps. How did they obtain so many stamps?

They bartered and traded for them on their own devised and effective inmate monetary system. They possessed extra stamps in some cases because of the dirty correctional officer supplying and selling them to the inmate(s) in the prison for their own selfish gain, only to be turned over to the administration usually by the same inmate at a later date when the inmate felt he had no use for the officer anymore because they had found a new officer to replace the other. Some of these stamps were delivered to the inmate through the inmate visitation system. A postage stamp is a very small item and is hard to find because the inmate knows how to secure them and protect their interest. Inmates sold and bartered almost anything they could turn over for a profit.

Another change that was complicated was removing the tobacco from the prison—a smoke-free facility. No snuff, smokeless dip or any other product that contained tobacco. This created hardship on all the inmates and the officers who smoked. All correctional staff could not smoke while on the job.

The program did afford some help to the inmates and staff with classes on tobacco cessation and afforded the inmates nicotine gum to help them quit. Most seemed to survive this change, but not all. Tobacco was still a problem in the prison as far as contraband was concerned. Inmates for years smoked roll-ups (make your own).

The brand was *tops* that came in a small yellow-and-blue bag. They bought rolling papers to roll them up.

All types of cigarette brands, dip, and roll-ups were removed from the canteens and were sold no more.

Every day, some inmate was caught smoking in the dorm, behind buildings, in the latrine, or anywhere they could try to hide. They would be charged and placed in segregation for a short time. Where did this tobacco keep coming from? It was being brought in by visitation and the inmate's best friend, again the dirty officer. Some inmates did not smoke but possessed tobacco they would sell to the inmates who continued to smoke. I believe without a shadow of doubt you could place one inmate on a building by himself with nothing but a cigarette and another inmate on another building across the prison with one match, and soon as you realized, the inmate who had only the cigarette will be smoking it. Sounds kind of far-fetched, doesn't it? Well, take my word that the inmate is very clever, and it is not that far-fetched. You can remove all money, remove the tobacco, remove their profit-making schemes, and they will come up with something in its place that will counter what was taken from them and continue to roll over a profit every day. If you do not believe this, don't fool yourself. They, by all means, are the most conniving, self-sufficient and extortionary individuals of deceit you will ever encounter. Not only did they continue to smoke with tobacco, they also smoked marijuana all the time. This drug was in the prison most of the time with the exception of certain dry spells. This substance has been found in ceilings, the dining facility, schools, maintenance, on the yards, and on the inmate. I remember one time the inmates were hiding their pot in the dining facility manager's desk without him knowing it. It has even been found stored in the tank of toilets in the bathroom. Then the problem of K2 started. This substance is very dangerous. It caused inmates to have seizures and ultimately end up in the hospital. By the way, the funding is coming out of your and my pockets for this unnecessary medical bill.

Inmates will continue to smoke and have a currency system even if the prison is smokeless and cashless. You can take that to the bank and draw interest on it.

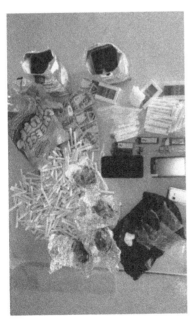

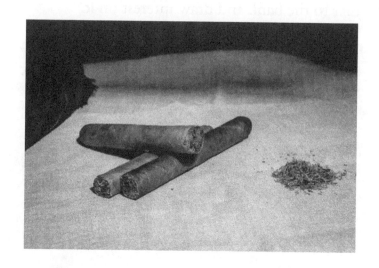

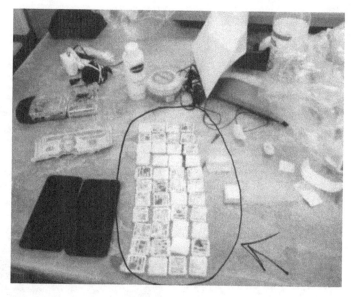

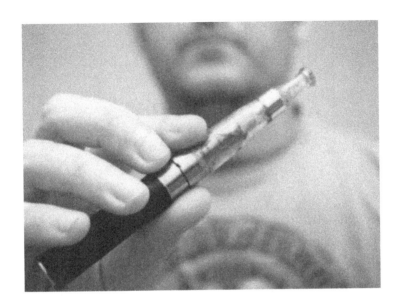

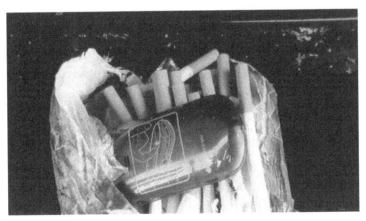

CHAPTER 11

Ramen
The "Oodles of All Noodles"

From the almighty dollar and various tobacco products, the taste of profit has changed in the prison environment. Due to the many changes discussed in my earlier chapters, inmates in the penitentiary have found alternate paths of self-wealth by manipulating the currency system.

Of all the ways to accomplish this method, it is mind-boggling to discover it comes in a small package of "oodles of all noodles," the good old Oriental ramen noodle.

The ramen noodle has become the *gold mine* within the prison. It is a small package of dehydrated noodles and a seasoning pack that is packed full of calories and excessive salt yet is so demanding and very lucrative. Every inmate has these noodles in their possession for their own consumption and especially for monetary cashless purposes. These noodles are prepared in many ways from the original package.

From rolls, swells, fried, or mixed with peanut butter, chocolate, crushed peanuts, and oatmeal to create something referred to as poo-poo balls, these noodles were broken in small pieces and placed in a microwave oven, only to toasted to delight that was worthy of fighting over. It was unbelievable, but I witnessed this foolishness several times. One of their favorites was mixed mackerel (fish) or summer sausages, cheese, chili beans, diced pickles, onions, chips of all brands, and a bag of dehydrated rice. These items were available in the canteen for their purchase. They will also use anything that they can steal from the prison dining facility. They roll all these ingredients into a soft tortilla shell and sell them for a profit on the yards.

The prison stopped frying chicken and other food products by implementing a baking process to ensure the inmates got better nutritional meals and to help cut back the cost of medical expenses. However, such items as the ramen noodle are heavily stocked throughout the commissaries and canteens, and though the ramen noodle is very unhealthy, it is the inmate's highest commodity for profit in the prison system.

As I walked through the dorm on a late afternoon, I saw three inmates in the dayroom making what they referred to as ramen burritos or rolls. All three inmates had put their purchases together in an effort to eat and sell them.

As I watched this small manufacturing progress, I was amazed at the knowledge they had in taking packs of ramen noodles, summer sausages, large pickles, chili, chips, cheese, and rice and go to work like a bunch of busy bees in a honeycomb. I noticed several packs of cut-up onions, chopped chicken breast, and small packs of spices and some hot peppers. I approached their operation and took a better look at the chopped chicken, onions, and spices. These items were contraband because they were not sold in the canteens. These items were from the dining facility. I confiscated the items, and they were not pleased.

As far as the inmates making their own food, it was not against policy; however, the contraband was. They showed their disapproval of me taking the contraband by their little nasty remarks, but I did not care what they thought or said. Each inmate knew they were in violation for possessing any contraband, and I could have stopped the whole operation so they continued preparing their food without any further remarks or issues. The spices, chopped chicken, and onions were returned to dining facility for proper disposal.

About two hours later, they had made at least thirty to forty of these burritos or rolls with the exact amount of food items they purchased from the canteen.

Nothing was left over and no waste.

There was no way three inmates could eat this many large burritos or rolls. The rest went for sale on the yards for profit or to pay off a debt. The problem was you could not prove this—no telling how many packages of ramen or stamps they collected for their efforts. Inmates will give or share with other inmate's food at any time, for this is not against prison policy.

How can the officer distinguish between the food sold or the food being given away? You can't! The ramen noodle rolls or burritos will continue to roll.

One of the most fascinating things, yet this did not surprise me, was what I observed while I was in the supermarket shopping for groceries a few months back. I happened to notice an inmate whom I knew was in prison who had been released and had completed his time. He immediately recognized me and did acknowledge my presence by nodding his head at me. Upon looking at his shopping cart, I noticed very few groceries and guess what? He had three or four large boxes of ramen noodles in his cart. I chuckled, for it only solidified what I believe to be the truth. Prison may help a few inmates when they return to society; however, most inmates, even after being released, have been so institutionalized while being incarcerated their habits will never change. I guess you cannot teach an old dog new tricks.

This is one of the main reasons there is such a recidivism rate among the released from prison. The Department of Public Safety and Corrections needs to ensure the prison departments do a better and more efficient job in preparing the inmate for entry back into society prior to them being released from prison. After an inmate or convict serves their time in prison for several years, providing them with only a small gate check and turning them back into society do not help them adjust to this new lifestyle, thus causing most of them to return back to prison within just a short time. I have known inmates in prison who came back for the third or fourth time. This should not happen on the large scale it does. But having worked there for many years, I understand why it happens.

To fully understand and determine how an inmate is doing financially in prison was to look into their wall locker and personal possessions and see the amount of canteen items and food they have. I would watch an inmate draw forty dollars from his account and spend most of his money on these tiny, small dehydrated fried noodles. Sounds a little stupid but was far from what you think. The amount of ramen noodles they possessed was the ultimate indicator that the inmate is doing well and even better if he bought a few postage stamps along with the noodles.

The question one should ask is, Why are these noodles being sold to the inmate in prison due to their monetary value and especially due to the health of the inmate? The only answer is because it makes money for the prison. It is lucrative for them also.

The overall health of an inmate is important due to the high cost of their medical bills. What is the effect on their bodies when they eat this type of food?

Because these noodles are so available in the prison, convenient, quick to prepare, cheap, and tasty, they have become the delight of every inmate. Is it bad for the inmate's health? I believe there are a few things that can happen to one's body when they eat these noodles. You can decide for yourself.

1. *Do not fully break down after hours of digestion.* Due to the added preservatives, the noodles remain intact after hours of consumption. This puts a strain on their digestive system, which is forced to work harder because of this being a highly processed food.
2. *Longer exposure to possible toxic additives.* This can cause extreme bloating. These noodles are very low in fiber and move slower in the digestive system.

This gives the feeling of a person being full with the feeling of being bloated when eaten in excess. There can be problems with these noodles due to the amount of MSG, which can impact brain health. MSG in studies can cause headaches and even nausea.

3. *Increase in body weight.* These noodles are high in carbs and in fat. Each pack of noodles contains approximately 7 grams of fat and 27 grams of carbs. These noodles can become addictive and cause weight gain.

4. Increased risk of heart disease, stroke, and type 2 diabetes. These noodles are full of salt. This affects the blood pressure, hardening of the arteries and leading to several major health issues.

With the problems of ramen being used as a monetary system and the overall health reasons, they should have been removed from the prisons already.

However, this is a lucrative business for the prison, and as long as there is a profit for both the inmate and the prison, ramen will continue to be sold. One would believe the health of the inmate is not a priority, only the money it generates.

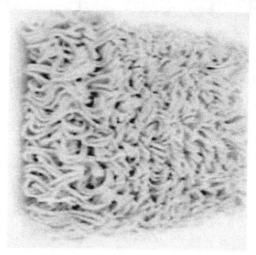

CHAPTER 12

Due Process and the Rule of Law

In this great country of the United States of America, everyone is presumed to be innocent until proven guilty by a court of law. In our society today, that is far from the truth. The politicians on the left are pushing their Progressive agenda and could care less what due process or the rule of law is. This was evident in the last confirmation hearing conducted for our newest Supreme Court justice, the Honorable Brett Kavanaugh.

The fake news media made it look as if they were not biased yet, at the same time, were in total support of the Progressive left in trying to tarnish and ruin this man's life. I believe in our great country's Constitution for how it was written and what it stands for. It has not changed; only the radical politicians have.

Everyone should be given their day in court without any political interference. If we cannot, as a nation, come together in a righteous manner as a "nation under God," then how can anyone believe there is a fair and justifiable system in our nation as well as our prison system. I will tell you, there is not. If these political hacks cannot agree with their colleagues to fix something as simple as our immigration system, the prisons in this country will continue to be overcrowded by the number of criminals breeching our porous borders every day.

It has become a malignant cancer that will continue to grow until the system is overhauled.

Being retired from the military, I am also concerned for the Uniform Code of Military Justice (UCMJ).

Even the court system in the greatest military in the world is being influenced by the fake news and political views (what a tragedy). Many individuals serving our country are being unfairly treated and prosecuted due to the lack of fairness and due process.

The prison system is in no way different. The disciplinary system is structured by a set of policies and procedures. However, even in the prison, what is good, for the "goose is not necessarily good for the gander."

This is mainly due to selfish political reasons. The prisons are kept full because it generates money for certain selfish individuals and does not care for the rehabilitation of offenders. There is no such thing as true rehabilitation in the prison. True rehabilitation comes from deep down in one's heart and soul, not any program established by the prison. I am a firm believer of this. I have witnessed several inmates get out of prison who you think have been rehabilitated by the system, only to commit crime again and go back to prison, serving longer sentences.

Certain inmates in prison violate prison rules and violations that are worthy of being placed in the segregation (hole) and get off scot-free, while some other inmates might do something so minor and end up serving over twenty days in the hole. Again, this is due to the unfairness in the system. I witnessed inmates get time in segregation (hole) just on a rumor that was not proven. So much for due process. The disciplinary system is extremely biased, totally broken, unfair, and needs fixing. Due to the administration and their political views, they have become so complacent and could care less about fairness. It is appropriate with them as long as it does not affect their social status and their position or get in their own selfish ways.

Inmate conformity to prison rules is absolutely necessary for the orderly, safe, and secure operation of correctional facilities. Effective, fair, and consistent disciplinary procedures enhance the orderly operation of the facility and reinforce appropriate behavior and responsibility. Prisons shall promulgate inmate conduct rules and disciplinary procedures and sanctions for all new admissions to the prison system and make them available in conspicuous locations within each correctional facility. Inmate disciplinary policies and procedures shall be reviewed annually and updated if necessary by a prisons chief disciplinary hearing officer (NC DPS Chapter B, Section .0201).

All inmates whose offenses result in a guilty disposition will be assessed an administrative fee of ten dollars through the Inmate Banking module of OPUS. Only one fee per disciplinary report is to be assessed regardless of the number of charges or number of reinvestigations. All administrative fees will be electronically collected through Inmate Banking and transferred to the general fund (Section .0203).

Inmates, when found guilty, get a ticket or, as I call it, a fine. They are charged ten dollars. The problem and unfairness with this practice is if an inmate is indigent and has no money and they are not fined because you cannot remove money from an empty bank account.

Although at the same time, if an inmate is fortunate enough to be supported by their friends or families and do have money in their account, it is there for the taking. Whether an inmate has money or not should not be the reason for the prison system taking money from them. They both are incarcerated and doing time for their crimes and are awards of the prison system. The prison department should not be in "the business of issuing citations" but in the business of providing safety, protecting the public, and assisting the inmate in becoming a productive citizen in today's society if or when they are released from incarceration.

Every inmate incarcerated should have the opportunity to work in order to help repay society for the cost of their incarceration and take a burden off the taxpayer. Most inmates just lay down and receive *three hot meals a cot* each and every day. Most of them have an attitude that the prison owes them something. If the inmate is physically and mentally capable, they need to work. The prison system should pay the inmate a minimum salary. Their salary should have food, housing, and medical expenses (a certain percentage) deducted from their earnings and the remainder be put in a savings mechanism for their personal use. This not only teaches responsibility and finances but also keeps them busy during the days. If they are tired after working all day, they will most likely go to bed and not be up gambling or causing issues.

Nothing is free in society and should not be in prison. The inmate will always use the term "It is my right."_What a true statement. You do have the right to pay for your own room and board, food, and medical just as any law-abiding citizen has the right.

As an inmate, what rights did you take from your victim or their family members? The saying "I have rights" is only a crutch the inmate uses to obtain what they want. Although when they use this as their crutch, the department often caters to them in fear.

Fear of what? The potential of lawsuits.

In the prison disciplinary procedures, inmates are charged offenses and are divided into four different categories—class A through D, class A being the most serious and class D being the least serious (Section .0202 DPS Inmate Disciplinary Procedures).

An example of a (A9) disciplinary charge is committing an assault on a staff member by throwing liquids, (including but not limited to urine and feces) or spitting on a staff person. In prison, you can get up to sixty days in segregation, demotion from medium custody or medium to close custody, and loss of up to (forty) days sentence credits as applicable.

On the streets today on the outside, you have certain radical groups throwing liquids (presumed to be water) on the great policeman of our cities. The fake news would like you to believe this is due to frustration and unfairness; however, it is merely political in nature. If we put these

GLEN R. REED JR.

radicals in jail for sixty days, you would see an uprising and the fake news to go absolutely insane. They need to serve time, for this is a felony. An inmate gets time in segregation for throwing liquids in prison, but it is an excepted practice to throw liquids on the police in society.

It has often been said, "As goes our prison system goes our nation." Wake up. Get a grip on life.

CHAPTER 13

Turn Them Over and
Shake Them Down

It would normally be around 5:45 in the morning when shift change started. During the shift lineup, it would be announced that we were going to conduct a 100 percent unit shakedown after the feeding of the breakfast meal for that day. The entire prison completely shuts down from all regular operations, and the general inmate population, including all segregated areas within the prison, would be completely searched. All areas including vehicles on the outside of the prison were turned upside down for contraband and for any other items that were not authorized by unit policy and procedure. Inmates normally were never fooled or got caught off guard on these unannounced shakedowns. Inmates knew in advance most of the time. I wonder why! Of course, they were told by their inside source.

The yards would remain closed, and all inmates were locked down in their respective dorms to include the dining facility and all work areas. While feeding was going on, a few officers would go to the clothes house and round up several laundry baskets on wheels and several large mattress covers to place all materials and extra clothing taken from the inmates during this operation. All the inmate was allowed were four pair of pants and four shirts at any one time. It was not uncommon for them to have double the amount of clothing authorized. Extra clothing was always an ongoing problem. It was not uncommon to take extra clothing from inmates, and within the same day, they would have all the extra clothing back again. At times, an inmate would have extra clothing that was new and never been worn before. As I stated earlier, this was not surprising for what a few packs of ramen noodles or stamps could get you, not to mention other items such as special favors and even sexual favors.

Upon completion of searching assignments, the captain or lieutenant officers went to their assigned area and started the search process. The process for searching was normally the same format when arriving in your assigned area unless there was a need for change due to security or other risk factors. Some officers were assigned to other areas besides the dorms where the inmates were housed. A few of these areas were maintenance, dining facility, meat plant, gym, academic and vocational schools, boiler room, chapel, the outer- and inner-parameter fences, the yards, barber school, the clothes house, and other areas designated by the captain on the shift.

When arriving inside the dorm, all the inmates were told to exit all sleeping areas and bathrooms and go immediately to the dayroom. All inmates would stay in the dayroom until they were individually called by name, have their prison identification card checked against an authorized dorm roster, and had completely finished their individual search. Upon finishing their search, they would be told to go on the yard, weather permitting, and were not allowed back in the building until the whole dorm had been completely searched.

The first sequence of events was to escort the inmate to the bathroom after having his identification verified. The inmate would then be directed to strip down completely naked to his "birthday suit" (strip search). This was to ensure they had no contraband, new tattoos, or apparent medical concerns. This was referred to as a complete full body search. This procedure was uncomfortable and degrading to some inmates, except for those who had been in prison for some time. The inmate would have to show the bottom of his feet and hands, remove any headgear, and shake their hair loose. They were required to open their mouths so the inside could be visibly looked out.

Probably the most embarrassing or uncomfortable part of this entire procedure was when they were told to lift certain parts of their anatomy, turn around, squat, and cough. The reason was to disengage any object that might be hidden in their body. A few would think it was funny and stick out their tongues and just laugh. But most of them had become accustomed to this procedure after a period of time. These practices were always accomplished with the same gender of the officer and the inmate.

After the completion of the body search, they were then escorted to their respective bed and wall locker area.

Their lockers were opened. The officer(s) would search the entire locker and bed from the top to the bottom. All items were placed back into the locker as they were looked at unless, for some reason, it was placed on the bed for further need. Some officers chose to place all their items on his bed after being searched. This took some knowledge and expertise in what to look for and where because of the time frame. For example, you need to search their boots and shoes in particular for hidden items such as keys, and even cell phones that_have been found in their boots or shoes. During the search, if the inmate refuses to comply with the search, they are placed in restraints, and their area is still searched. You would be amazed at what you might find during these searches—contraband such as money, extra stamps, pornography (magazines from the outside), marijuana, weapons, extra clothing, radio parts, extra canteen such as those from many ramen noodles, tattoo guns, needles, and medication from another inmate and not of their own authorized prescription. These are just a few. I once found inside the steel-toed boots of an inmate a set of keys for the dining facility during one search. This inmate did not steal these. I will let your imagination try to figure out how they were obtained.

One method the inmate was known to employ was to hide their contraband around and near to their sleeping area. When this contraband was found on shakedowns, it was determined not theirs because under the bed, in plain sight, and not hidden were considered to be in a *common area*. This usually came down to a judgment call by the administration but normally was found to be in favor of the inmate.

I once found a bar of soap in its original box during a search. The bar of soap had been used by the inmate. Upon breaking the bar of soap in half, I noticed it had been hollowed out on the inside with a twenty-dollar bill folded and placed inside the soap. The bar of soap was placed back into the box and sealed, making the soap look as if new and never opened. The money in the soap had been put back together with water, making the bar of soap look as if used.

Books were another means to hide their desired contraband, especially schoolbooks and the *Bible*. The book would have all the pages on the inside cut out in a square where they would place their contraband in the cutout area and then close the book. It was not uncommon to find small, dime-size packs of marijuana tightly wrapped in cellophane and stuffed in the cracks between the top of a window and the walls of the dorm and dayrooms. They would even hide these items inside the toilets wrapped inside a rubber glove to keep from getting wet. They would hide contraband in board games such as Monopoly, Risk, Dominos, and Checkers.

One contraband that you would normally not expect to find in the morning was alcohol. This particular morning, at shift change, while conducting count, my partner and I smelled something strange in the bathroom. Upon searching the bathroom, we discovered inside a large garbage can hidden under a bunch of dirty clothes a large trash plastic bag filled with prison-made liquor. This concoction was often referred to as a buck). This prison-made liquor was mostly made of oranges, apples, bread, and other fruits along with yeast stolen from the dining facility if they were fortunate enough to get their hands on it. Buck is extremely nasty and crude but very potent and profitable. This particular batch of prison buck was exceptional. You could tell by the strong alcohol odor. The trash bag containing the buck was so heavy we had to obtain a cart from the yard in order to remove it. Their party time was busted again! The confiscation of the buck usually did not upset the inmate, for they were always making another batch somewhere. You could bet a drink on it!

Another type of search that was performed several times during the day and night was the routine (PAT) search. This was a systematic search where you would start from the top of the inmate and end at the bottom or from the bottom to the top of the inmate.

This was normally where you inspected pockets and waistline and patted the inmate down. This particular type of search was used for exiting and entering of all areas, for spot checks, and prior to going on an approved visit.

The complete full-body search (strip search) was used during the exiting of an approved visitation, prior to being placed in segregation, removal from the cell, and for any other security reasons. Searches may seem to be intrusive at times but are required and are necessary tools used to control the flow of contraband and provide protection and security to all inmates and correctional staff.

Let the "roundup begin and shake them down."

A complete an effective search goes without questioning because this correctional tool is and will always be necessary.

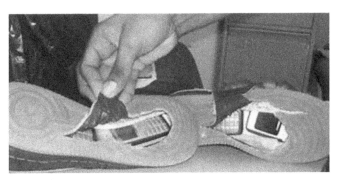

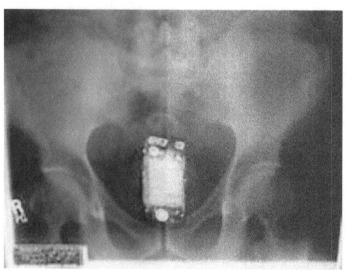

CHAPTER 14

The Walls of Babel

From the very beginning of time, man did not have trouble communicating with one another. The scriptures tell us that all men and women spoke the same language at one time. While they were living in the city of Babylon, man decided he was going show off his "great city" and, in doing so, would build a tower that would "reach the heavens." This was referred to as the Tower of Babel (Genesis 11). This, however, did not please God, so God himself confounded the languages of the world where they were not able to communicate with one another, causing great division among the human race. Since that period in time, man has had to learn to communicate with their own language and has had to learn other languages in order to fully understand one another.

This is no different in the prisons today. The inmates have established their own form of language and definitions for words they communicate with.

They scramble their words, so they are able to communicate to one another without the correctional staff fully understanding them. I refer to this as the gibberish called prison babel! It takes some time as a correctional officer to learn and understand these definitions. For the most part, this is universal within most prisons, with some minor exceptions. The use of these words is sometimes based off the Urban Dictionary (a community-powered dictionary of slang terms). An example from the Urban Dictionary is *po-po*. This term normally refers to policemen, correctional officers, or other law enforcement officials.

Slang terms are a normal way of life for the inmate.

It's not natural—something they are born with—but something learned. It is mind-boggling that most inmates cannot fully communicate without using slang or some form of vulgar vocabulary during their conversations. This is another example of one being a product of their environment. Most of this is due to their education, family background, and the crowd they dealt with prior to being incarcerated. Using profanity is a violation in the prison system especially if it is directed to correctional staff. In most cases, they have even developed their own prison language that only they understand among themselves. But normal prison babel was used in their everyday communication among themselves.

Some of these terms are used in other prison systems but have a different meaning. This depends on the area you have been in.

Here are a few babel terms used by most convicts and inmates in the prison today. You will possibly hear some of these slang terms on the streets outside of these babel walls.

- *Browns*—prison clothing for medium-custody inmates
- *Greens*—prison clothing for minimum-custody inmates
- *Red jumpsuits*—prison clothing for death row inmates
- *Brown down*—drop from medium to minimum custody in type of clothing
- *Hootch/pruno/buck*—prison-made liquor
- *Hole/seg*—segregated housing
- *Yard*—recreational area
- *Snitch/narc/bitch*—an informant inmate
- *Nickel*—five-year sentence
- *Dime*—ten-year sentence
- *Smell gas*—trip or work on the outside of prison
- *Girl/punk*—homosexual
- *White shirt*—captain or lieutenant
- *Fe-fe*—prison-made sexual device for men
- *Suitcase*—to have placed contraband in the rectum
- *Gun*—prison-made tattoo machine or man's sexual organ
- *Ink*—tattoo
- *Ink pusher*—inmate who does tattooing
- *Dotted up*—to have received a tattoo
- *Roll-up*—cigarette
- *Blunt*—cigar / cigar paper

- *Cell*—cell block
- *Pc/check off*—protective custody
- *Chow*—dining facility
- *Visit*—visitation
- *Blue shirt/po-po*—correctional officer
- *Soup*—ramen noodles
- *Jac mack*—mackerel fish in can/pouch
- *Gig*—job
- *Homie*—inmate friend from same town or area
- *New jacks/cowboys*—new correctional officers
- *Dirty*—dirty correctional officer
- *Fish*—new inmate to system
- *Brogans*—prison-issued boots
- *BO-bos*—prison-issued tennis shoes
- *Chester*—child molester
- *Hawk*—lookout inmate for other inmates
- *Flags/stamps*—postage stamps
- *Shiv/shank*—prison-made knife
- *Ticket*—disciplinary report
- *Double nickle*—(2) razor blades in toothbrush weapon
- *Throw gas/gassing*—urine, feces, body fluids thrown on officers
- *Catch a ride*—get high off another's drugs
- *Dotted up*—tattooed
- *Gunned*—masturbated on an officer
- *Dry snitching*—talking loudly about another inmate in front of correctional staff
- *Kite*—passing of notes from one inmate to another
- *Piss test*—urine tests for inmates

- *Turtle suit*—blanket used while in suicide watch
- *Buck-fifty*—cut on face that requires to get at least 150 stiches
- *Dry cell*—a cell block with no plumbing and water
- *Unit manager*—supervisor who oversees a large group of inmates
- *Shot caller*—high-ranking gang member with power to order hits
- *Soldier*—gang member who carries out given orders
- *All day*—a life sentence
- *Brake fluid*—psychiatric medications
- *Bug*—staff member considered untrustworthy or unreliable
- *Bug juice*—intoxicants or depressant drugs
- *Diesel therapy*—long bus ride for being transferred for being a trouble inmate
- *Chin check*—to hit on to see if they will fight back
- *Duck*—staff who reveal information to inmates about other staff
- *Doing the dutch*—to commit suicide
- *Fire on the line*—a warning of staff in area
- *In the car*—in on a deal or plan
- *No smoke*—to follow staff orders without resisting or creating problems
- *On the bumper*—trying to get in on a deal
- *Peels*—orange jumpsuit
- *Prison wolf*—inmate who normally is straight on the outside but engages in sexual activity with men while incarcerated

- *Ride with*—To do favors for your fellow inmate
- *Roadkill*—cigarette butts picked up from roadside
- *Stainless steel ride*—death by lethal injection
- *Knee deep*—to stab one but not to kill them
- *Wolf tickets*—talk tough but never back it up

There are many more. As a correctional officer, it is imperative for you to communicate with others and especially the inmate. In order to function effectively each and every hour you are behind these walls, one must listen, take notes, and learn.

Every opportunity as a correctional officer, I would make it my top priority to listen, jot down these terms, and remember what they meant and how they applied to the environment as a whole. I always carried a small book in my pocket that I recorded all incidents, times, my work schedule, inmates' use of words and phrases, and any particular issue that I felt was pertinent to the job for the safety of my coworkers, the public, and myself. In order to survive the prison environment, it is imperative that you learn their language.

CHAPTER 15

Don't Smile; You're Paying the Bill

Each day after getting out of bed, we take our shower, brush our teeth, get dressed, eat breakfast, get the kids off to school, and then go to our place of employment to begin another day of work.

Things are not as easy today because of the high cost of gas, food, mortgage payment, car notes, and medical insurance. Let's face the facts. If we do not generate some form of income, then we possibly would not eat or have a roof over our own heads. In my father's and mother's generation, they normally came from larger families with at least nine or more siblings. This is definitely not the case today because the cost to raise a family is much more demanding and expensive.

As Americans, we will always pay taxes. This is understandable and is a necessity in order to keep our economy and cities functioning. The issue with most taxes is they are so high and not necessarily due to the greed and corruption within our own society. One of these is our judicial system. I believe it's necessary to place individuals in prison for certain crimes they commit in order to keep society safe. But how long does one need to stay in prison for issues as minor as simple drug use, petty theft, and nonviolent crimes, creating the overcrowding of the prison system and placing a larger tax burden that all citizens pay for these extraordinary bills. The tax burden on you and I is astronomical!

The immigration system in this country is out of control due to Progressive politicians. We have lost control of own our borders and cannot monitor who is illegally entering into this country, contributing to the cost of incarceration of these undocumented immigrants, and the taxpayer ends up supporting them. I am frustrated and extremely concerned about these self-righteous liberal politicians who only care about themselves and not the American people. These politicians need to search their hardened hearts, wake up to what is reality, or go back home and secure a normal job at McDonalds or Wendy's, sell Kirby vacuum cleaners, or work in a tobacco field during long, hot summer days for what the minimum hourly wage is. This might wake them up, but this is below their greedy standards.

The cost of corrections in North Carolina is as follows according to the North Carolina Department of Public Safety (DPS) (ncdps.gov.adult-corrections\cost of corrrections).

North Carolina has fifty-six (56) prisons that house around 38,000 inmates. The prisons are divided into four regions—Central, Coastal, Mountain, and Triangle (en. wickipedia.org/wickilist of North Carolina-State Prisons).

The Cost of Prison Incarceration for Fiscal Year Ending
June 30, 2018
Costs Per Inmate

	Daily	Yearly
Minimum Custody	$86.92	$31,726
Medium Custody	$102.46	$37,398
Close Custody	$116.75	$42,614
Average	$99.23	$36,219

If you take the average cost per year of $36,219 × 365 days, this figure comes to $13,219,935. Quite a burden on the taxpayers. The story doesn't end here.

The additional costs of areas such as community supervision, substance abuse, probation, parole, and many other programs keep the amounts growing.

Another large sum of money is the salaries for correctional officers, training, and uniforms. Just in correctional officer uniforms alone, I saw three (3) different changes over my tenure. This is costly because the employee doesn't pay for their own uniforms; the administration picks up the cost up at your expense again. In the military, I had to pay for my own uniforms at my cost, not the government's.

The prison department has many programs for the inmate to assist them in becoming a better person in society upon their release. Some of these programs are worthy, and some are not, but all are at an expense. The one program that is worthy of its expense is the GED program. Every inmate who does not possess a high school diploma should get one. In fact, this should be a mandatory requirement for every inmate prior to being released from incarceration. It is difficult to find a job without a high school or a GED equivalency today. Releasing someone without basic education only adds to the problem of recidivism. A convicted felon who has a substantial amount of time to serve should not be afforded a college degree. There are law-abiding citizens on the outside who work hard and cannot afford a college education. To offer an inmate a college degree while incarcerated is totally ridiculous, unfair, and a waste of the taxpayers' money.

Another program that I feel is a total waste of time and money is a program that attempts to rehabilitate sexual offenders (SOAR program). This program is about twenty-two weeks in length and, in my opinion, is a total waste. An individual who is incarcerated for having been found guilty of a sexual crime with a minor or child will never be fully rehabilitated. These criminals should not have the opportunity to attend this type of program. They should remain in prison and not be allowed to enter society for the entire duration of their sentence. While working as an officer in this particular environment, I found in the inmates' possession during a routine search items such as elicit pornography and other sexual materials while they were enrolled and attending this course. Their minds are deviant, and if they get back on the streets, they most likely will offend again. They might wait a few years or more, but they will most likely hurt some child or young person and ultimately end up back in prison. You might not agree with me on this issue, but until you have seen and worked around these types of criminals, you have no idea how they think or what they are capable of doing. These inmates are even despised by other inmates in the prison. They actually hate them. They refer to these sexual offenders as chesters or child molesters.

It takes a large amount of money to operate and maintain a penitentiary. A lot of unnecessary and fruitless programs exist. At the costs associated with incarceration, this cost could be lowered if the excess fat was removed. The inmates have needs just as we do; however, they are incarcerated, and only their required needs should be met, not their wants and desires. One should ask, Does the entire prison system need to be overhauled and the laws changed?

The cost of maintaining and operating the prison system is overbearing, and it steals from a society that is law-abiding, but we are only fooling ourselves by robbing and cheating the "good citizens and giving it to the criminal."

CHAPTER 16

The Revolving Door of the Correctional Officer

What does it take to be an effective and productive correctional officer in the prison system? This is a difficult question that deserves a good answer. First of all, I am not a psychologist in today's modern society who feels they have all the answers. The answer to this important question normally comes from an individual or group think tank that has never darkened the gates inside of a penitentiary or ever experienced working with incarcerated individuals.

To answer this important question is extremely difficult, but having being on the inside of this difficult, diverse, and perverse world of walls and razor wire fences for over twenty-two years, I believe it is so simple yet so difficult to explain.

Not every person is able to handle this type of work environment. It takes a woman or man who is mentally and physically able to bear the mental anguish and abuse from some of the most ruthless, cruel, and mentally unstable individuals who have been graciously removed from our society, individuals who have committed rape, murdered the young and old, committed arson, became sexual predators, robbed banks, and abducted young children for their own deviant pleasure, and the list goes on. To be an effective correctional officer, one must possess the attributes of good character, honesty, wisdom, and loyalty; possess good communication skills; be financially stable; and fully understand what the difference between apathy and sympathy is. Above all, this special individual must possess great amounts of intestinal fortitude. They must be fair but firm in dealing with this type of population. This is just one of the many reasons why there is such a large turnover rate of personnel in this extremely dangerous work environment.

Stress, the silent killer, is extremely dangerous and plays a large part in the workforce today. The duties of the correctional officer are extremely stressful. It has been said that this occupation ranks among the top 5 occupations of stress-related issues today. Stress can affect your health before you even realize it. Other officers have told me that their stress caused them headaches, insomnia, acid reflux, overall change in behavior, and an evident decline in their job performance. This is a serious issue since stress has been known to possibly lead to heart disease, hypertension, diabetes, obesity, and even suicide in some instances.

Age is a factor as well. Individuals who are in their early twenties seem to fail out of this occupation at a larger and faster rate. They are still young, and being placed in a secured area full of adult inmates is more than they can handle. A lot of inmates are old enough to be their parents or grandparents. In no way am I discriminating; it is just a fact of life. And yet the human resources departments within the prison administrations continue to believe this age group is conducive to the safety for others and the protection of the public. I have witnessed too many times a new correctional officer who comes to work today and is gone tomorrow. They just cannot handle the pressure and stress of this environment. Again, this occupation is not for the weak or the weary.

One afternoon, I was working down the bottom area of the prison when two officers came into my area escorting nine or ten new officers on their new-hire orientation. I had the opportunity to talk to a few of them and noticed a few of them shaking in their shoes. This is natural for the first time. The point I am getting to is, in only a few days, there were only a few left. The others had quit and never came back. Why is this?

Within the Department of Public Safety, there are standards for the hiring of correctional officers and staff. Just possibly, they are broken and need some revision. If these standards were revised or followed as written, there would possibly be less officer or staff shortage within the prisons. The staff-to-inmate ratio is unequal and devastating to the welfare of the officer, staff, and the general public in most prisons today. Oh, by the way! Do not blame it on staff salary alone. The pay is far better today than when I worked those long twelve-hour shifts.

This is a common concern, but the effective hiring and screening standards of potential correctional officers are paramount. I read an article the other day where a correctional officer was under investigation for dealing with an inmate. It was discovered later on that this officer had a past criminal record. What about the background check completed on this individual prior to being hired? I guess it just slipped through the cracks! Better hiring practices and standards by human resources usually equal better correctional officers and staff. The present turnover ratio will decrease, and the retainability of good officers will increase.

I realize that even when all the hiring standards have been met, this does not guarantee the potential hiring of an individual means they are going to stay or even be a good officer. Other situations cause the turnover problem other than just the hiring system.

Over the years, I worked and observed many officers get escorted out of the prison for dealing with inmates, bringing in contraband, having undue familiarity with an inmate, having sexual issues with inmates, and many more. They become dirty. Over my time, I saw over one hundred officers being escorted out of the prison for these types of reasons. The most difficult situation I never understand was when a seasoned officer with many years of experience on the job gets tangled up in the trap of a convict, and the end result was them losing their job and retirement. Like I said before, only the strong survive.

Not only officers but also case managers, chaplains, psychologist, doctors, maintenance workers, and nurses have let the influence of an inmate or convict cause them hardships and embarrassment and eventually end up becoming unemployed. In the prison, you will always find dirty employees. These individuals are dangerous and become a security risk to everyone who works in the prison. Each and every dirty employee just lost their job but should have been prosecuted to the full extent of the law.

Due to these circumstances causing staff shortages, it makes the good officer's job more difficult. Many times, while working on shift, we would have less than forty officers for an inmate population of almost one thousand. An inmate once told me the "the prison runs smoothly because we allow it to run smoothly." There is validity to this statement. Just think again: forty officers to almost one thousand inmates. The odds are not too good. I knew of an officer who lost their job because he purchased parts for his watch on the internet, then illegally brought them into the prison and had an inmate repair the watch for him for a small fee and favor. Another officer lost his job for having an inmate draw a portrait of his own family. These sound kind of minor, but it is wrong and against policy. They should not work in the prison. Why would you show an inmate a picture of your family? This is just plain ignorant and possibly putting your family in jeopardy.

Small things create big problems. Not only do they give the inmate the upper hand, this also affects the overall safety of the environment by losing an employee and having to replace the vacancy. This takes some time and is costly.

Treatment of staff and correctional officers is another reason for shortages for employee turnover. Each shift is supervised by a captain and lieutenant. These two individuals make major decisions that affect the staff and inmates on a minute's notice. In some cases, certain officers were treated better than others. This included prefer-ence on where you were assigned to work each day. Some officers were better at certain jobs than others, but this created issues with other officers. This had an impact on staying in the prison system. Some officers did not like to work on the gun towers or the yard but found themselves assigned there every day. They would quit because they felt they were not being treated fairly by working positions that were not favorable and should have been rotated on a daily basis. One example is having to work outside in the extreme heat and cold every day while another officer worked inside an air-conditioned building, such as medical or in the dormitories.

Requesting time off for vacations always seemed to be a thorn in the side. Due to the number of officers needed to run the shift, thus causing shortage of staff, vacation and compensatory time-off requests were denied when requested on a regular basis. For the most part, you were told when you were able to take off from work. This cre-ated a pattern of officers not asking for the day off only to call in sick the day they needed off. The policy stated you could be out for two consecutive days without having to bring in a doctor's note for being sick. However, I have seen where an officer was told by the lieutenant on shift to bring in a doctor's note for being out just one day. This cre-ated animosity and also was against policy and procedures. Many factors caused turnover, but the administration was their own worst enemy.

According to a recent article that was posted on September 24, 2019, and updated on September 25, North

Carolina would temporarily have to close three prisons due to staff shortages. The article stated that more than one-fifth of the correctional officer positions in fifty-five prisons were vacant. The article went on to say that staffing problems were a contributing factor in an escape in 2017 from one prison that left four prison workers dead. The redeployment of staff to other prisons nearby and the moving of an estimated 1,500 inmates to other prisons would take place over the next four to six months, a spokesman from the state Department of Public Safety stated.

The article went on to say that this would not cause overcrowding. Moving 1,500 inmates across the state to other prisons is very dangerous when you do not have adequate manpower, and they are only putting a Band-Aid on a major wound (www.Staff Shortages force NC to temporarily close three prisons/18655750/).

Just recently, a television show WNCN 2Min Read-NC stated correctional officers leave as fast as they were hired, officials say.

In 2018, DPS hired 1,812 correctional officers, while 1,742 left. The vacancy has a ratio among correctional officers at 20.6 percent according to the data provided by DPS.

The most common issue or problem employees stated in exit surveys was the workload and lack of adequate staffing. They also cited inadequate compensation, unsafe working environment, lack of say in decision-making, scheduling, and lack of career development. It also stated that they were allowing all those inmates out, up to 150 inmates, for one or two officers to maintain control of and to watch for oversight purposes. A correctional officer who spoke with CBS 17 earlier this year said, "We're outnumbered drastically." The program went on to say the agency is also seeing high rates of vacancies in medical and mental health. This is not a problem that should continue to be overlooked; this a dangerous situation.

In this type of employment, you are always going to have issues that creates the shortage of staff, but with a little more prior planning and the ability and desire to work with people and identifying problems of stress, I honestly believe the administration could lower the "bleeding of staff turnover" if they so desired. The prison is not a business as some believe it to be.

CHAPTER 17

Politics in Prison

Just Because Your Shirt Is White
Doesn't Make You Right

Every organization or business has a structured system for everyone, starting with the CEO down to the last employee. It is no different within the prison department.

Over the years I was associated with the prison system, they always referred to this structure as their chain of command. There was no chain of command because the administration controlled everything that went on behind the closed walls and fences. The administration used this military clique quite frequently. They had no idea what a chain of command was or will ever be. Let me explain.

The administration wanted to use some form or fashion of structured leadership patterned after the way the military does it. It doesn't and will not work in the prison environment. Labeling your leadership as sergeant, lieutenant, captain, and warrant officer is not feasible in this sense. An employee who had been promoted or elevated to one of these positions had no control or authority other than what was outlined in the prison policy or allowed by the administration's political view.

The prison department used a standard form of uniforms by their set policy and standards. The officers all wore the same style of uniform. The only exception were lieutenants, captains, and the dining facility manager, who wore white shirts. The lieutenants controlled everything that went on during their assigned shift. Their call was final. Some questions were not asked, or you would not be considered part of the good old boy system.

The sergeant was merely a pawn used by the lieutenants, captains, and the administration. The stripes meant nothing. However, when things went wrong, they were held accountable. "Just because your shirt was white didn't make you right." I had the opportunity to work with many outstanding lieutenants during my tenure; however, many were scared of the system and the inmate and hid behind their white shirt. Many used their position for their own political gain and movement up the ladder. I was often frustrated but managed over the many years to keep my composure and not let this interfere with the safety and protection of the inmate and/or the public. The good ole boy system was the political mechanism used by anyone who wanted to move up their chain of command, not caring who they hurt or stepped on.

Politics is nasty especially when it comes to being treated the same and having the same opportunities as other employees. Your political affiliation, whether it is Republican, Democrat, or independent, should have no bearing on your job or keep you from progressing through the many different opportunities of one's career. Sorry, but it is a fact. I remember one day I was asked by the superintendent of the prison if I was a registered Democrat. He personally told me in a shopping center (Food Lion) one evening outside the prison that I would never get very far in *his* prison system. I was working in the capacity of an acting sergeant for three years and never got promoted. I still performed my job.

It is no different in today's society. It is sad that one can only hope and pray things to change for the better.

This type of corruption is what is causing problems for this great country of ours today—one political party who thinks they are above the law and can do what they want.

How can the Congress of this country fix the basic issues within the prisons when they cannot even fix the problems such as immigration, which is a major contributing factor to our overcrowded prisons? The lying, corrupt, and fake news doesn't even care because of their own political agenda.

It all comes to one major issue, and it doesn't matter if it is in the prison or outside of the prison. As long as we have individuals who are so far on the left and so progressive who care only about themselves and not doing their jobs for the great people of this God-fearing country, the "inside of the prisons in the United States of America today will become a reality of what the outside of America could become tomorrow". It has been said, "Rome fell from the inside, not the outside."

If we continue to allow the rule of law to be changed and destroyed for political reasons by the Left Progressives and small interests' groups lining their pockets with corruption, greed, money, and scandals, our streets will eventually become modern-day battlefields. Look at the problems of the homeless and drug abuse use on our streets and in the prisons today. Look at San Francisco, California. It's a crying shame. Our Congress in power today has done little to nothing the past three years but conjure up extreme hatred, promote lies, and attempt to ruin our great leaders and veterans, such as General Flynn (thirty-three-year veteran).

They have accomplished nothing for the people of this country. If the Speaker of the House (Congress) as well as the leaders in our prisons today continue down this road of political deceit, our prisons and this great country will be headed for hell in a hand basket. "And if a Kingdom be divided against itself, that Kingdom cannot stand. And if a House be divided against itself, that House cannot stand" (Matthew 12:24–25).

CHAPTER 18

Frustration of Rehabilitation

Merriam-Webster dictionary defines the word *rehabilitation* as the "action, process of rehabilitating or of being rehabilitated." This is the process of restoring someone (such as a criminal) to a useful and constructive place in society—the rehabilitation of prisoners—a prison rehabilitation program. This is the restoration of something damaged or deteriorated to a prior condition.

There are many theories and constructive programs today to assist an individual through a structured rehabilitation program. This is evident in the prison system today. Most rehabilitation programs have evolved into time and excessive expense. The prison system is no exception. The rehabilitation in the prison system is costly and requires a lot of time working with convicted inmates and convicts both with either violent or nonviolent convictions.

Rehabilitation should be top priority, but the success rate is extremely low in prison. It doesn't matter what type of program, how long, and how much, for there is no rehabilitation unless the inmate or the convict purposes in their own heart, mind, and soul that they truly want to be rehabilitated. Unfortunately, this just does not happen in most cases.

An individual will not experience true rehabilitation until they take full responsibility of the crimes and acts they have committed. Most inmates and convicts are in self-denial. This is evident in the recidivism rate in prisons as discussed earlier in a prior chapter.

Unfortunately, research has consistently shown that time spent in prison does not successfully rehabilitate most inmates and convicts. The majority of criminals return to a life of crime almost immediately upon release or parole from incarceration. Rehabilitation of prisoners is an extremely difficult process. The process of rehabilitation should begin from the moment of incarceration and continue even after release or parole. Incarceration is not meant to be pleasant. The combination of ineffective prison guidelines (policies and procedures), budget shortages, and an unfair punitive philosophy of corrections has made the prisons in our society today unpleasant, unsafe, and less effective in rehabilitating the inmate and convict.

Inside the Department of Correction/DPS, many programs have been implemented for this reason. Some programs are good, with the majority of them a waste of time and a burden on all, including the taxpayer.

A few of these implemented programs are the following:

    a. SOAR (sexual offender accountability and responsibility course)
    b. Think Smart

c. Road Crews
d. Narcotics Anonymous (NA) and
    Alcoholics Anonymous (AA)
e. New Lease on Life
f. Bridge
g. Inmate construction program
h. Napoleon Hill
i. Residential substance abuse program

The substance abuse treatment program is a prime example of rehabilitation not working. An inmate or a convict who has been in prison for many years for selling and distributing drugs and has been convicted as a drug dealer is offered this particular course. After being paroled or released from prison in just a short time, they have been caught selling drugs again and sent back to prison. Rehabilitation at its finest. This is not true of all individuals incarcerated for drugs, but the success rate is extremely low.

During my tenure as a correctional officer, there was one particular inmate who was assigned as the dorm janitor in the area that I was assigned to on a regular basis. This inmate had been incarcerated for over ten years for multiple crimes, including the possession and the distribution of drugs. He had taken all classes in the areas related to his past crimes to assist him in some form of rehabilitation. He was considered a model inmate who was highly respected by his peers along with most of the correctional staff.

Upon his release from prison, he returned to his hometown. Within a short time later, he was caught stealing from his own family, who supported him through his prior years in prison. He then proceeded to fall back into his prior lifestyle, being convicted by a court of law and finding himself back in prison for a large period of time. This is one example of why rehabilitation is so frustrating in the prison system. As I stated before, the blame does not completely fall on the prison system for failure in rehabilitation because one must purpose in their own heart before true rehabilitation can become effective.

Inmates and convicts who worked on Road Crews normally worked five days a week, weather permitting. Inmates worked on Road Crews picking up trash along various roads and highways, helping keep the highways clean, but this did not in any way help them in the area of rehabilitation. Do not misunderstand me, for the inmates and convicts need to work and not just lie around all day. These particular inmates love the chance to get outside the prison fences. They use the term, "Let's smell some gas." This refers to working outside of the prison where they can look at cars, people, and society while picking up trash on the roads.

Rehabilitation is frustrating in the prison, but the system needs to try to work harder at the opportunities they can give to the incarcerated.

More time needs to be spent on educational opportunities in the prison. Inmates and convicts should not be allowed to lie around, lift weights, play basketball, and do nothing. They all need to be in some type of activity that challenges their pattern of thinking and opens their eyes so that, just perhaps, some form of rehabilitation will become effective. Although keep in mind that some will never become rehabilitated no matter what the prison system does.

As a last thought, I believe the one and true way an individual becomes completely rehabilitated is through their faith in God, our creator. God can and will clean the heart of all mankind, including the most heinous and ruthless individuals in our prisons today if they just ask him for forgiveness. Again, true rehabilitation comes from repentance and purposing in your heart that you want to change. The prison system cannot completely change a person's heart.

ABOUT THE AUTHOR

Glen is a son of a military family with a combined service of over forty-three years in the United States Army.
He served in several countries and troops, including the
Republic of South Korea (The United Nations), the US
Army Garrison, and the Second Infantry Division. He
completed several tours in Europe with the Eighth US
Army. Upon retiring from the military, Glen began a new
career in the field of adult corrections within the penitentiary system for the next twenty-two years before finally
retiring. Presently, he is working part-time in the field of
substance abuse. He graduated from Lawton Senior High
School in Oklahoma. During his time in the military, he
took several college courses that enabled him to obtain his
degree in criminal justice. He lives outside Fort Bragg in
Fayetteville, North Carolina.

CPSIA information can be obtained
at www.ICGtesting.com
Printed in the USA
JSHW011449270920
8260JS00001B/21